D0886979

GOD,
MAN AND
BASKETBALL
JONES

BY THE SAME AUTHOR

GOD, MAN AND BASKETBALL JONES

THE THINKING FAN'S GUIDE TO PROFESSIONAL BASKETBALL

BY

CHARLES ROSEN

HOLT, RINEHART AND WINSTON · NEW YORK

PUBLISHED BY HOLT, RINEHART AND WINSTON, 383 MADISON AVENUE,
NEW YORK, NEW YORK 10017
PUBLISHED SIMULTANEOUSLY IN CANADA BY HOLT, RINEHART AND
WINSTON OF CANADA, LIMITED.

LIBRARY OF CONGRESS CATALOGING IN PUBLICATION DATA
ROSEN, CHARLES.
GOD, MAN AND BASKETBALL JONES.
1. BASKETBALL—UNITED STATES.
2. BASKETBALL PLAYERS —UNITED STATES.   I. TITLE.
GV885.7.R65   796.32'3'0973   79–11512
ISBN 0–03–43991–4

FIRST EDITION

DESIGNER: AMY HILL
PRINTED IN THE UNITED STATES OF AMERICA
1 3 5 7 9 10 8 6 4 2

WITH LOVE, FOR RUDY AND LISA,
AND ESPECIALLY FOR MY MOTHER

GOD,
MAN AND
BASKETBALL
JONES

JUMP BALL

It's a prime-time National Basketball Association play-off game: the Los Angeles Lakers hosting the Portland Trail Blazers. Starring 7'4" Kareem Abdul-Jabbar, with his devastating sky-hooks and his unexpected storklike grace. And featuring 6'10" Bill Walton, the red-bearded wizard of the redwoods.

The contest is tense, dynamic, and brilliantly played. Abdul-Jabbar is at the top of his game, but neither team is able to sustain an advantage. With only twenty-nine seconds left to play, Abdul-Jabbar cans a pair of free throws and puts the Lakers ahead 97–96. Portland immediately signals for a time-out, and the two ball clubs huddle around their respective coaches. The Blazers' coach, Jack Ramsay, hovers for a moment. Then he crouches to one knee and holds a miniature basketball court in his left hand. The television camera zooms, and forty million people watch Ramsay's lean fingers weave five magnetic chips through the play he wants his team to execute. Then the strategy dissolves into a beer commercial. . . .

"If you don't drink this stuff," says a glowering ex-football player, "I'm gonna break your nose."

We are returned to the Fabulous Forum just in time to see

1

Portland's Lionel Hollins inbound the ball to teammate Herm Gilliam, who takes two sharp dribbles and lobs a high pass to Bill Walton at the foul line. The camera zeroes in and frames Walton and his defender, Abdul-Jabbar. "Mountain Man has the ball," says the play-by-hype announcer. "Twenty seconds left. Nineteen. The clock is counting down." The fans at the Forum are rabid with anxiety, and armchairs are gripped tightly in living rooms from Harlem to Honolulu. But Walton calmly clamps the ball at chest level and protects it with a flash of his elbows. "Twelve!" says the announcer, his voice rising. "Eleven! Ten!" Walton waits another beat; then he suddenly wheels and throws a perfect bounce pass offstage left. The surprised camera backs up and reveals Herm Gilliam all alone, a mere 10 feet from the basket. Gilliam has ample time to clear his throat before banking a jump shot off the backboard and through the hoop. The Lakers have already used their last time-out, and a desperation pass is thrown away at the final buzzer.

It was a great game. Even the newspapers said so. But somehow—despite the obvious delights—large portions of the game were confusing and unsatisfying. Particularly the grand finale. Where, for example, did Gilliam come from? Why wasn't anybody guarding him? And who's really better? Walton or Abdul-Jabbar? Budweiser or Schlitz Light? It's easy to blame the one-eyed TV monster for everything. But most of the fans in the stands would have trouble answering the very same questions. The simple truth is that we all have been trained by the media to follow the bouncing ball. Most of us do not see enough of a pro ball game to fully understand its unfolding. We lack sufficient information to gauge a player's performance accurately. Nor can we convincingly indulge in the fan's most cherished prerogative—second-guessing the coach. We are conditioned to look where the camera points, and we miss about 80 percent of every NBA ball game.

"I've spoken to the network people about this many times," says Dave Cowens of the Boston Celtics. "They claim that the fans demand to see the ball. Now, I'm not saying there's anything wrong with that. There's obviously a place for the ball in basketball. Kids are always ball-conscious. Things like shooting, dribbling, and passing offer immediate gratification, and basketball should be fun when you're young. It should always be fun. But there are also parts of the game that are strictly for the serious players and the serious fans."

Basketball is indeed a game of high seriousness. Like many other athletic encounters, basketball offers much more than rousing entertainment. The game has inspired novelists, metaphysicians, sociologists, fanatics, and saints of both the schoolyard and the barnyard. The game has spawned TV movies, commercials, and mega-$ contracts. Its players are nothing less than culture heroes—"Dr. J," "Pistol Pete," "Super John," "The Big E," "The Big O," "Wilt the Stilt," "Tiny," "Clyde," and "The Black Jesus."

Basketball is one-on-one and burn-on-burn.

Basketball is ballet with defense.

Basketball is a blur of acrobatic giants, perilous abandon, and ram-slam-in-your-mother's-eyes dunk shots.

And for even the most casual fan, basketball can also be a dribbling, leaping, flowing salvation.

1
24 SECONDS TO SHOOT

Professional and college basketball are as different as soft-boiled and scrambled eggs. All professional sports have an inescapable element of the bizarre, but the college basketball scene reeks of hypocrisy, grand larceny, and petty morality. Schoolboy hotshots are recruited with dollars, ladies, credit cards, wheels, and tales of glory. There have also been at least two occasions where the athletic departments of major universities have supplied heroin to junkie All-Americans. "Everybody's got goodies to offer a kid," says a veteran college coach. "It all comes down to how you spread your wares. It means getting in there and bullshitting some eighteen-year-old kid who has a head as big as a basketball. You tell the kid he's going to be a star. You tell him he's going to live on Easy Street for the next four years. Most of the time the kid doesn't have a chance. There's no way your promises and his expectations can ever live up to the reality of big-time college basketball. And a lot of kids, especially the inner-city blacks, get very angry very easily."

A dissident college basketball player can usually be tamed in a hurry: His gratuities can be terminated. His playing time can be curtailed, disallowing any expectations of a pro career. A recalcitrant player can also be placed on "waivers": His "private tutors" can be recalled, leaving him liable to academic ineligibility and the revocation of his scholarship.

The options available to the unhappy ballplayer are much less effective: He can go back home. He can hang out at school and go through the motions. He can drop out and get a job. He can change his ways. Or he can try to make a connection with another school. It's usually no trick for an authentic "blue-chipper" to come to agreeable terms someplace else. But he has to forfeit a full semester of athletic eligibility, and he gains a lasting reputation as having "an attitude." The end result is that most college basketball teams are direct extensions of the character and philosophy of their coaches: Adolph Rupp's University of Kentucky Wildcats ran the same fast break from 1930 to 1975, while Pete Carril's Princeton Tigers have been slowly working the ball along the same dotted lines for the past eleven years. Legend has it that Nat Holman once berated a CCNY player for daring to deviate from an offensive pattern when his defender turned an ankle and fell to the floor.

The college game boasts of an incomparable enthusiasm and the constant possibility of fantasy. But college basketball is susceptible to overcoaching, delays, stalls, and freezes. The legal use of zone defenses also tends to make college offenses mechanical and cautious. There are obviously a great many dedicated coaches who know that coaching and teaching are the same thing. But the powerhouse college basketball coaches have a stranglehold on the players, the media, and the game. The college game is too self-conscious to be well balanced. . . .

Gene Shue is coaching the Baltimore Bullets. He sends rookie Stan Love into the ball game to replace an obviously tired veteran. The insulted veteran hovers over the bench and points his complaints at his coach's face. "Fuck you, Shue!" the player says. The other ballplayers guffaw, but Shue just shrugs and takes his seat. . . .

NBA basketball is unquestionably more accomplished and more spontaneous than the college variety. Most NBA ballplayers have fame, fortune, and tenure, and the tone of a normal pro team is influenced more by the players than by the coach. Perhaps the pro game is less restrained and more natural because all the money is laid atop the table. But it's the sheer speed of the pro game that really makes the difference. Velocity always creates pressure—on the athletes, the coaches, the referees, and the fans. On all those who would measure, regulate, or analyze the game. And the rapacious speed of professional basketball also serves to obscure the true nature of The Game.

Since 1954 speed has been mandated in the NBA.

The harbinger of the NBA was the Basketball Association of America, formed in 1946 with franchises in Boston, New York, Philadelphia, Providence, Toronto, Washington, Chicago, Detroit, St. Louis, Cleveland, and Pittsburgh. Strictly a bush league. During the BAA's initial '46–'47 season, the keystone New York Knickerbocker franchise was allowed only six playing dates in Madison Square Garden. The Knicks played the remainder of their home schedule in a renovated U.S. armory. Over the same season the Garden allotted twenty-eight of its choicest dates to college basketball doubleheaders. Nothing could illustrate more clearly the comparative importance of college and early professional basketball. The pro game was sufficiently skillful and brutal to have mass appeal, and the point spread made gambling fun. But the sports public viewed the professional hoopster as a hireling.

Eddie Gottlieb, the charter owner of the Philadelphia Warriors, observed the financial success of the Harlem Globetrotters and became convinced that basketball fans would gladly spin the turnstiles to witness something freakish. So Philadelphia aimed its offense at 6'6" Jumpin' Joe Fulks, and the Warriors became a solid gate attraction. Fulks was the founding father of the jump shot, and he scored the unheard-of total of 41 points in a ball game against the Toronto Huskies. Fulks went on to average 23.1 points a game to lead the BAA in scoring. By comparison, Bob Feerick of the Washington Capitols finished a distant second with 16.8 per game. Fulks's salary was estimated at $15,000, the average player received about $5,000, and many players were paid by the game. Yet only a handful of franchises escaped heavy financial losses that first season.

In addition to being subordinate to college basketball, the BAA was competing for attention with another pro circuit called the National Basketball League. The NBL's meal ticket was 6'10", 250-pound George Mikan out of De Paul University, a high-scoring dreadnought who lived in the shadow of the backboard. Mikan would steam across the foul lane, leaning and blasting his way into spinning lay-ups and unstoppable hook shots. The prodigious Mikan led the NBL in scoring in '46–'47 with 16.4 points a game.

The rival leagues struggled for another season, losing money and playing musical franchises. Then, in the summer of 1948, the BAA raided the NBL and came away with the Rochester Royals, the Fort Wayne Pistons, the Indianapolis Jets, and George Mikan and his Minneapolis Laker playmates. In 1948–49 Mikan averaged 28.3 a game, while the Lakers cruised to the BAA championship and drew SRO crowds wherever they went. Whenever Minneapolis played in the Garden, the marquee always read: TONIGHT'S EVENT—GEORGE MIKAN VS. THE KNICKS.

The NBL gasped for another year but was forced to submerge into the BAA just in time for the '49–'50 season. The brand-new National Basketball Association featured seventeen teams in three unwieldy divisions. Ten teams played a 68-game schedule, four teams played 64 games, and three teams played 62 games. All but five of the teams qualified for the play-offs. Even with Fulks, Mikan, and a growing stable of talented players, the fledgling NBA remained a bush league.

Zone defenses were outlawed from the start, but an early NBA ball game was just as apt to be tedious as exciting. Teams consistently got easy shots by slowly working the ball to their shooters or into their big man. The New York Knicks were traditionally the runts of the league and were forced to play a running game because their centers were 6'6" Harry Gallatin and 6'5" Nat Clifton. But for the rest of the league, there was no real percentage in the fast break.

A pro team with a sizable lead had no incentive to try to increase its margin. If they did play normal aggressive offense and then missed the shot, the opponents were handed an unnecessary opportunity to close the gap. Just as in college basketball, the leading team would often resort to a stall and have a clever dribbler freeze the ball. "Sometimes it got to be silly," says Red Holzman, a player with the aboriginal Rochester Royals and later a championship-winning coach of the Knicks. "I can remember a ball game when we started freezing the ball very early in the fourth quarter. One of the players got so bored that he actually sat down on the court and read a newspaper." The trailing team was faced with the prospect of either letting the game wind down into a surefire loss or playing reckless defense. Then, as now, recklessness is invariably translated into personal fouls. Before the team foul limit was instituted, it also made sense for a losing team to trade a single free-throw attempt for the chance to score a basket (and perhaps even a 3-point play). The players habitually committed this type of foul with a heavy-handed violence that often left the foulee groggy. Either way—the slowdown strategy or the relentless parade to the foul line—a pro game was frequently a sluggish affair. The novelty of high-scoring players soon began to lose its flavor, and even the hard-core fans began staying home.

On November 11, 1950, the situation seemed to come to a head when the Fort Wayne Pistons defeated the Lakers by the score of 19–18. George Mikan tallied a game high of 15 points and took 11 of the Lakers' total of 18 shots. The visiting Pistons attempted only 13 shots from the field. A bare fortnight later the

Rochester Royals played an infamous five-overtime game against the Indianapolis Olympians. Each extra period began with a jump ball, and the team that won possession simply held the ball and attempted a win-or-draw shot at the buzzer. The first four overtimes were scoreless, and only the hired help remained to see the Olympians finally hit a basket in the seventy-third minute of "play" to prevail, 75–73.

The game was moribund, and something drastic had to be done.

Then, in January 1951, the first in a series of revelations of widespread fixing of college basketball games came to light. When all the news was out, a total of thirty-two players from CCNY, LIU, NYU, Manhattan, Bradley, Kentucky, and Toledo admitted conspiring with gamblers to rig almost 100 ball games over a span of four years. The kiss of scandal changed the college game into a frog and turned the hirelings into "honest professionals." Four of the tainted colleges were located in New York, and Madison Square Garden was quick to change its scheduling priorities: In '51–'52, the Knicks played 25 home games at the Garden, while the number of college double-headers was pared to 18. In addition, the Knicks' games were fitted into the most lucrative time slots of the week: Sunday afternoons, Tuesday evenings, and Saturday night in New York. The NBA's bylaws stipulated that the home team retained all gate receipts, and the pivotal New York franchise suddenly turned to gold. . . .

"Me and my buddies were already basketball junkies by then," says Snaggletooth Louie from a telephone booth in the back of a candy store in the Bronx. "When CCNY and LIU dropped their basketball teams, the NBA had the only decent game in town. Then the Garden started booking pro double-headers. It was terrific. Five hours of basketball. Indoors. With all your buddies and plenty of beer. And with college basketball in the dumps, the pro game was the only smart bet." . . .

The unexpected turn of events caused the NBA moguls to

abandon all plans of tinkering with their product, and the '51–'52 season was a box-office bonanza. During the next two years the league consolidated into two divisions and nine stable franchises. The outlook was bright; but the game still had the same old structural dead spots, and attendance soon sagged. In the summer of 1954 the NBA Board of Governors decided to commit the future of their enterprise to the establishment of a shot clock. Danny Biascone, the soft-spoken owner of the Syracuse Nationals, handled the final details, and 24 seconds turned out to be the magic number. It allowed a theoretical minimum of 123 shots per game. Yet it provided enough time to run a play and a half. And the diurnal number 24 also suggested the annihilating threat of a midnight buzzer.

A lone dissenting voice was raised by Max Winter, the owner of the Minneapolis Lakers. "The twenty-four second clock discriminates against George Mikan," said the outraged Winter. "It's like baseball legislating against Babe Ruth." Under the new dispensation, a team that had to set up its offense slowly and wait until its big man maneuvered into position would never have time left to run a play. But the new rule was put into effect for the '54–'55 season, and the NBA was off and running.

The emphasis turned to speed, intensity, stamina, and one-on-one moves, and every team had to master the fast break. As Max Winter suspected, the great George Mikan was a front-line casualty. Mikan announced his retirement before the '54–'55 season began, and he became the Lakers' general manager. Big George sat out the entire season, but when the Lakers lost 15 of their first 20 ball games in '55–'56, Mikan renounced his retirement. At the age of thirty-one, Mikan was able to recover his legs and his wind. Mikan played a few strides behind the rest of the league, but he still averaged a respectable 10.5 points over 37 games. Despite Mikan's noble effort, the Lakers finished with a losing season for the first time in history. Attendance rapidly declined, and the Minneapolis franchise never really recovered.

If George Mikan was a dinosaur, the NBA had a new generation of gate attractions: Neil Johnston, Dolph Schayes, Ed Macauley, Paul Arizin, Bob Cousy, Bob Pettit, Carl Braun, Bill Sharman, and Frank Selvy. Attendance was up all over the league, and most ball clubs could now afford to travel by airplane. In 1960 the Lakers moved to Los Angeles, and the NBA became increasingly glamorous and affluent: The league expanded into Chicago in 1966, and players' salaries soared to an average of $12,000 a year. Then the league signed a television contract. Wilt the Stilt scored 100 points against the Knicks early one Sunday afternoon in Hershey, Pennsylvania. Over the next few years the NBA branched out to Houston, Seattle, Portland, Phoenix, San Francisco, Cleveland, New Orleans, and Buffalo. In 1976 the NBA swallowed the American Basketball Association. Two years later the average player earned $143,000 a year, and professional basketball was a vital part of America's sports consciousness.

Despite the undeniable growth it spurred, the 24-second clock was not without its critics. Some fans said that the only part of an NBA game that really counted was the last five minutes. This view was ostensibly supported by an informal survey conducted by Bill Sharman, onetime Laker coach and current general manager. Sharman discovered that 40 percent of all NBA ball games are decided by 1 point, 2 points, or an overtime period. But to believe that an NBA game is won or lost only in the last few minutes is like walking in on the ninth inning of a double perfect baseball game and believing that you haven't missed a thing. The truth is that the 24-second clock made the majority of NBA ball games highly competitive from buzzer to buzzer. No lead was safe, and halfhearted play was always costly. The 24-second clock vitalized the NBA and put a charge into the game.

2
THE MEDIA AT THE KEYHOLE

The only way to find the Golden Key is to slow the game to a standstill: Full-court stop-action reveals that there are ten players on the floor but only one basketball. An occasional guard like Pete Maravich or Kevin Porter will monopolize the ball by design, but even if he plays the entire game, a theoretical player controls the ball only 4.8 minutes. "You can tell a lot about a player by what he does when he has the basketball," says Phil Jackson, a ten-year veteran of the New York Knicks. "Some guys have trouble letting go of the spotlight. Some guys want to follow the ball all around the court."

The official NBA basketball is a Wilson 10-XL. It weighs 20–22 ounces, is inflated to a pressure of 7½–8½ pounds, and has a circumference of 29½–30 inches. The seams are deep, and the leather skin is pleasantly pebbled. During its travels a basketball is bounced, thrown, slapped, seized, fondled, punched, kicked, and shot at the basket. Given their choice, most players would rather use it to shoot. NBA action usually generates 50 foul shots a game and about one field goal attempt every fifteen seconds. So the league's outstanding shooters are very obvious and very numerous. The NBA's lifetime shooting percentage is 46 percent and rising. But putting the ball through the hoop is actually the easiest basketball skill to learn, to practice, and to perfect. . . . When Mike Riordan was a number-twelve draft pick of the Knicks back in 1968, his jump shot was a brick. "Being a poor shooter was really a blessing in disguise," says Riordan. "I was forced to compensate, and I had to learn how to play basketball even when I didn't have the ball." Sheer determination transformed Riordan into a capable shooter, but he still spent most of his nine-year NBA career playing off-camera. Riordan currently owns and tends a successful bar in Annapolis, Maryland. "There's much more to offense than just shooting," he says. "I probably would never have made the pros if I was a really good shooter from the start."

Good shooting means good jump shooting, and the jump shot means instant points. . . . Joe Fulks, of course, was the first pro to display an effective jumper. Fulks's style was widely imitated, and such players as Paul Arizin, Bill Sharman, Ed Macauley, and Bob Pettit became the jump shot's leading practitioners in the early 1950s. Nowadays every player in the league has a jump shot. . . . At 6'4", Brian Winters is 3 inches shorter than his defender, Bobby Wilkerson. Winters has the ball near the top of the key; he fakes left, fakes faking right, and then jumps to find his shot. Wilkerson bounds after the ball, but Winters has already beaten him to the top. Winters launches the shot during that split-second "hang-time" before he starts to fall. His body is stable, his wrist is loose, and Winters's shot makes the net dance.

The jump shot can be shot off-balance, on the run, on a dime, and in heavy traffic. Over 80 percent of all field goals attempted in the NBA are "jays" of one kind or another. The rest are lay-ups, dunks, hooks, and assorted flips. But from time to time a player comes into the NBA armed with a trusty shot of his own invention: Kareem Abdul-Jabbar's "Skyhook," Wilt Chamberlain's "Finger Roll," Rod Thorn's two-handed jumper, George McGinnis and his hesitation one-hander, Dick Barnett and "Fall Back, Baby," and Walt Hazzard's "Leaping Leaner."

13

If the media has emphasized the shooters, it has canonized the dunkers. A few years ago the halftime TV carnival matched NBA players in a "Slam-Dunk" contest. Julius Erving sat out the competition, but there was still enough pageantry, spectacle, money, and instant culture to turn the dunk shot into a touchdown. "Dunk shots are strictly show biz," warns Bill Fitch, coach and general manager of the Cleveland Cavaliers. "It's best to forget about them and get on with the game. But the players sure do love to throw it down. If I could dunk, I guess I would, too."

In addition to showing off, some players utilize the dunk shot as a sign of disrespect. "A dunk on a breakaway doesn't mean a thing," says Bob McAdoo of the Celtics. "It only counts when you do it into somebody's face." All the fancy dunk shot artists are black—Julius Erving, David Thompson, Darryl Dawkins, Larry McNeil, Richard Washington, Dan Roundfield, and Darnell Hillman. Through the years, there have been only a few good white jumpers—Joe Fulks, Jim Pollard, Gene Conley, Ron Reed, Billy Cunningham, Bobby Jones, and Glen Gondrezick. Black players who can't "sky" are said to have "white man's legs" or "the white man's disease." But the real secret of a good dunk repertoire is having strong hands.

In 1966 the august National Collegiate Athletic Association announced a prohibition on dunking in all games under their jurisdiction. The ruling was explained as an attempt to level the overwhelming influence of the big men, but many observers felt that the ban was racially motivated. In any case, the injunction wasn't repealed until 1976. There's no doubt, however, that the dunk shot can indeed be habit-forming and hazardous to a player's equilibrium. . . . In 1977 Darrell Griffith was a 6'3½" guard for Louisville University, a first-team All-American, and a certain number-one pro draft pick. His game highlighted a 44-inch vertical jump and a sparkling array of dunk shots. "I designed the team's warm-up jackets myself," said Griffith. "They're black doctors' smocks with a red cardinal on the front. On the back is each player's nickname. And in big red letters there's the team motto—'The Doctors of Dunk.' My own nickname is Dr. Dunkenstein."

The professional dunksters can also get the bends when the media turns on the pressure. At the ripe age of twenty, Darryl Dawkins of the Philadelphia 76ers has the tools and the time to become the ultimate NBA center. Unfortunately it's far too easy for Dawkins to pick up media strokes by performing "Gorilla Dunks" than it is to try and stretch out his talent. The 76ers' public relations department has been tallying dunk shots for years and is forever pressing the NBA to include the category in the official league statistics.

Arnold ("Red") Auerbach is the NBA's resident seer, and nothing delights him more than resolving issues. His credentials date back to the primeval summer before the BAA's inaugural '46–'47 season. At the time Auerbach was a brash young man of twenty-nine and just recently discharged from the navy. Despite the fact that his only previous coaching experience was on the high school level, Auerbach buttonholed Mike Uline, the owner of the Washington Capitols. "Make me your coach," said Auerbach. "I know the game. And besides, I also know a lot of good ballplayers from the armed forces leagues. I can put together a competitive team cheap and in a hurry." Auerbach got the job. He coached his navy buddies to a 49–11 record, and the Caps won a divisional title before being eliminated early in the play-offs. Auerbach moved on to coach the Boston Celtics in 1950. Then, six years later, he traded Ed Macauley and Cliff Hagan for the rights to Bill Russell. Over the next ten years the Celtics captured nine NBA titles, and Auerbach developed a passion for victory cigars. "Roundball Red" retired from the bench in 1966, and as Boston's general manager he administered the Celtics to four more championships.

Auerbach knows that his physical presence is preceded by

the incontrovertible record of his genius, and he always speaks with authority. "I think the dunk shot is great," he says. "It showcases the grace, power, and imagination of the players. But it's all false stimulation. Only the media and the crowd gets a boost. . . . Yeah, I know. Some guys use dunk shots to insult each other. But no matter how the ball goes in, all you get is 2 points. There's no question that the media deliberately miseducates the fan and distorts the game. That's because the real name of the game is to put asses in seats."

The masters of the media agree that professional basketball is primarily entertainment, but the players aren't so sure. "I'm a basketball player," says Jim McMillian of the New York Knicks by way of Columbia University, "competing against the best players in the world. Of course it's entertaining. Basketball is the greatest sport there is. It's The Game. If the media wants to turn it into a circus, that's not going to change the way I see myself."

Perhaps the most blatant media manipulation in recent years was the 1966 NBA All-Star game. The ball game was played in Cincinnati, and the starting lineups included John Havlicek, Wilt Chamberlain, Bill Russell, Oscar Robertson, Willis Reed, Dave DeBusschere, Rick Barry, and Jerry West. The TV network decreed that the ball game's Most Valuable Player be given a car. All-Star games are always mindless and anarchic, and the players responded by hoisting up a near-record total of 238 shots from the floor. The outcome of the game was never in doubt, and the Eastern Division trounced the West by 43 points. Garbage time began early in the second quarter, and the most prolific collector of meaningless points turned out to be Adrian Smith, one of three Cincinnati players who appeared in the game. The delighted hometown fans cheered Smith's every move. Even though he played only twenty-six minutes, Smith finished with a game high of 24 points. As soon as the final buzzer sounded, the fans began chanting Smith's name. They applauded and threw paper cups when the MVP award was driven out to center court. Then they made threatening noises as the sportswriters counted the ballots. In order to avert what one writer called "an incipient riot," Smith was given the nod. The NBA brass was so alarmed by the incident that they insisted a trophy be substituted for the car in subsequent All-Star games. The troublesome Cincinnati franchise was finally shipped to Kansas City in 1972.

Then, in 1977, the league was persuaded to restore the presentation of a car to the All-Star game's MVP. This time the final score was close, but the ball game was still disorderly and lacking in intensity. Billy Cunningham was the coach of the East squad, and he was quick to register his dismay. "The media is doing everything it can to change the game into nothing but one-on-one moves," he said. "They're forcing the game away from the team concept, and they emphasize only individualistic skills. The media is hypnotized by the ball, and the game is being ruined."

The Media Muppets closest to the game are the sportswriters. Members of the press and the athletes they cover rarely talk about each other in terms of respect. Some writers see themselves as creative spirits and the players as ingrates. Interviews with dull and/or uncooperative players have to be enlivened to create good copy. Writing what a ballplayer "should have said" or creating an artificial context for what he did say is a common practice. "It's all fiction anyway," says Eric Lincoln, a prominent free-lance writer. Some sportswriters are diligent, talented, and compassionate purveyors of the NBA scene. Some are gossipmongers. Some are "jock sniffers."

As a rule, a ballplayer will never trust a writer. The players are convinced that the average writer knows little about the game. They cite the '72–'73 season, when Dave Cowens ran rough-shod through the league. Cowens averaged over 20 points, 16 rebounds, and 41 minutes a game. He played kamikaze defense and powered the Celtics to a regular season mark of

68–14. Cowens's season-long freak-out won him the votes of his fellow players, and he received the Maurice Podoloff trophy as the NBA's MVP. Meanwhile, back in the press room, the writers neglected to elect Cowens to either the first or the second NBA All-Star teams.

"Writers are very strange people," says a hoary veteran of the NBA. "They're obviously intelligent, yet they all ask the same stupid questions. They take the most offhanded things you say and then blow them totally out of proportion. But they also lie a great deal, so it's always easy to bullshit them." Some players are actively hostile: The peerless Oscar Robertson would often shout down any sportswriter who dared to laugh at a joke he had intended for the ears of his teammates. There are some players who believe everything they read about themselves and who revel in the public eye: Harold ("Happy") Hairston was fond of roaming the Hollywood bars wearing his Los Angeles Lakers sweat suit and carrying his equipment bag. There are also ballplayers whose suspicions about the Fourth Estate approach paranoia. But for the most part, writers and ballplayers are careful not to antagonize each other. The writers need to keep their sources of information flowing freely, and most of the players value the exposure. Newsprint, interviews, and prime-time film clips can bring instant recognition to a player. Any agent worth his salt can easily turn that recognition into big bucks.

Most media people swear that nothing is as safe as a percentage, and nothing is as objective as a number. So the media evaluates professional basketball players solely on the basis of statistics. With few exceptions, the official NBA stats register what happens only when a player comes in contact with the ball—shots, rebounds, assists, turnovers, steals, blocked shots, and free throws. "Personal fouls" presumably record what happens when a player comes in contact with another player. "Games" and "Minutes Played" are absolutes (although a one-second appearance is counted as "one minute"). But the final score is the only relevant number, and win or lose, Red Auerbach swears that "NBA statistics are a fraud."

When Ernie DiGregorio was the White Hope of the Buffalo Braves, the hometown scorer would present him with an assist practically every time he touched the ball. In a home game played against the Knicks during DiGregorio's rookie season ('73–'74), the Braves scored 42 baskets and were credited with 39 assists. On one particular play, Ernie D. received an inbounds pass and dribbled over the midcourt line, where he passed the ball to teammate Jim McMillian. McMillian faked several times and then dribbled the ball for at least five seconds. The shot that McMillian finally found was good, and Ernie D. got an assist. When Kevin Porter was with the Washington Bullets, he was once credited with two assists in forty-one seconds. But it was later discovered that the Bullets went scoreless during that stretch. Red Auerbach tells of an NBA player who was given three assists even though he was sitting on the bench.

The players claim that individual scoring totals are also a sham. "White players are protected by the officials," says an NBA player who insists on anonymity. "So they get to shoot many more foul shots than they really deserve. If you sneeze near Gail Goodrich, they'll whistle you down and send him to the line. White guys also get extra rebounds and extra assists." But black players can likewise be the beneficiaries of an official scorer's largess: When the Washington Bullets hosted the New Orleans Jazz in the final game of the '74–'75 regular season, Wes Unseld needed 30 rebounds to surpass Dave Cowens and capture the NBA's rebounding title. Unseld's total for the night was puffed up with tips, taps, and deflections, and he finished with 30 on the nose.

Even when they are scrupulously tallied, rebounds can be an especially deceiving category. The NBA took a significant statistical step in 1973, when it separated offensive and defensive rebounds. All offensive rebounds are jewels, but how many of a player's defensive rebounds include the uncontested recovery of missed free throws? Most ballplayers are very conscientious about keeping track of their own statistical accomplishments, and they will always complain bitterly whenever they think the official stat sheet has cheated them. Unsuccessful taps are usually scored as missed shots on the road and as rebounds at home. According to several players, Milwaukee is a particularly tough city for a visiting player to receive an accurate account of rebounds.

Depending upon the fortunes of the home team, there are times when a regulation game lasts more than forty-eight minutes and times when it runs less. "The only statistic you can trust," says Red Auerbach, "is a ballplayer's free-throw percentage. All the rest are jerked around." Another deterrent to precision NBA statistics is simply the continuous and precipitous speed of the game. For a variety of reasons, the soul of a basketball game is never laid bare by a box score.

A field goal is always worth 2 points, and a free throw is always 1 point, yet there is an alternate method of scoring a ball game. "I used to figure it this way," says Jerry Sloan, now an assistant coach of the Chicago Bulls. "My aim was to get eight rebounds, draw four offensive fouls, and pick up three loose balls every game. If I was successful, that's a total of fifteen times I could give my team possession of the ball. In the NBA, each possession averages out to 1.1 points. So without even taking a shot, I could still contribute 16 points to the ball club."

A catalogue of impressive statistics can turn any player into a "superstar" and fill his life with: universal admiration, glass walls, fawning agents, flattering friends, willing women, cocaine, divorce, arrogance, and the satisfaction of every whim. ... Gus Johnson had a diamond inlaid into a front tooth. Wilt Chamberlain's bedspread is made of wolf noses. Kareem Abdul-Jabbar played a monster from outer space on a television series. Jamaal Wilkes and Happy Hairston are bona fide movie stars. "The star system in the NBA is based mostly on scoring," says Jack Marin, an eleven-year man and twice an All-Star. "I guarantee you that good looks have nothing to do with it. Most people don't realize that any player in the league can be a big scorer if he's set up to get shots. But I guess that people like having their public idols. Maybe it fills some kind of void in their own lives."

Whatever the reason, the Superstar Syndrome is endemic in the NBA. Once the disease strikes, a player's game will immediately show signs of deterioration. It makes no sense for a high-scoring millionaire to coast on offense, but playing earnest defense does entail a definite risk, that is, a rash of personal fouls that can limit playing time and shrivel point totals. "A guy like Bob Lanier has incredible talent," says Larry Brown, coach of the Denver Nuggets. "But like most of the other superstars in the NBA, Lanier doesn't come to play every night." The consensus seems to be that the average NBA superstar produces one intense ball game for every three he plays.

"It's so hard to keep your balance," says Jim McMillian. "Most NBA players have been superstars since high school. They've been pampered monsters since they were eighteen. I was lucky because I never played basketball until I was sixteen and I had a wonderful coach. But the pressure is always on. I think the media is mostly responsible for a recent decline in the quality of play in the NBA. There are more and more guys coming into the league who are not sound ballplayers. Guys who are useless without the basketball in their hands. It's depressing."

Some players have developed a "shadow-line" persona to deal with the media and keep it at double arm's length. Some seek isolation. A precious few manage to live untouched in the eye of the media cyclone. . . . Dave Cowens is a redheaded frontiersman. He is a hardworking, soft-spoken individualist. Cowens lives in a rented cabin and drives a battered pickup truck. "Basketball is such a public game," he says, "and the media grabs for every angle it can get. But I think it's wrong for professional athletes to be granted such tremendous prestige and power. Playing basketball is not a very important occupation. I think people should be admired for what they are, not for what they happen to do for a living. That's why I think it's foolish for people to crowd around and beg for my autograph. My lousy signature on a piece of paper is meaningless unless you really know me and decide that I'm an admirable person. It's not such a good thing either for little kids to think I'm such hot stuff just because I'm a basketball player. It's the same when sportswriters want to do articles on me. I get embarrassed. I think of my family and my friends back home, and I wonder if they aren't better people than I am, if the articles shouldn't be done on them instead. But in this business, if you don't sit still for interviews or sign a lot of autographs, you get a bad name."

No matter how much a player resists, the media always leaves its mark. Basketball players are too big to hide, and they are the most visible of athletes: They are singularly unprotected by helmets, masks, or hats, and they wear nothing but fancy underwear. They are as distinctive as Bill Walton's beard, Willis Reed's scowl, Phil Jackson's shoulders, Slick Watts's head, Bill Bradley's baggy pants, Jack Marin's birthmark, George McGinnis's muscles, and Zaid Abdul-Aziz's bald spot.

Whatever the angle and however close the close-up, the media is at best an inadequate guide for the "serious" basketball fan.

3
CIVILIANS IN SNEAKERS

If the media and the stat sheet can distort the game, then the NBA's corps of referees can drive a reasonable man to distraction. Joe Lapchick was a venerated member of the Original Celtics. Even his opponents praised him as a gentleman. Lapchick later moved on to St. John's University, where he earned a reputation as a master coach and a minor saint. But from 1947 to 1956 Joe Lapchick was the head coach of the New York Knicks. . . . Dick McGuire, the Knicks' flashy young guard, has the ball above the foul line. His man gives him plenty of room to shoot, but McGuire is looking for teammate Vince Boryla to flash through the pivot. "Shoot!" the fans scream, and McGuire fakes a quick two-handed set shot. Boryla is bumped to the floor as he starts his cut, and once more the crowd yells "Shoot!" McGuire's next two-handed twitch lifts his defender to his toes. McGuire suddenly ducks and darts to the hoop. Just as he releases an easy lay-up, McGuire is blasted off his feet by a 6'9", 250-pound hit man named Don Otten. The shot bites the rim too soon and bounces off the backboard and into Otten's waiting hands. The referee inspects the play, sucks his whistle, and runs downcourt to follow the ball. Joe Lapchick jumps to his feet, fuming, protesting, and gargling with anger. As he wheels and strides to the water cooler, Lapchick dips into his pocket and pulls out a handful of change. Without saying a word, Lapchick flings the coins at the feet of the offending referee.

In the early days of the NBA a ref's hide was always in season. The officials were publicly maligned by scores of coaches and owners and an occasional ballplayer. This state of affairs continued unabated until Ben Kerner, the owner of the old St. Louis Hawks, realized that the squabbling was doing the league no good. "Knocking the officiating," said Kerner, "is like having the most expensive restaurant in town and then standing on the sidewalk in front of it, yelling, 'My chef stinks!' " The NBA's Board of Governors was quick to see his logic, and an automatic fine of up to $1,000 was established for any player, coach, or owner who publicly questioned the infallibility of the league's game officials. The ruling successfully gagged the owners, but the coaches' rage continued to spill over into the newspapers: In Willis Reed's rookie year as coach of the Knicks ('77–'78), his persistent salvos at the refs cost him more than $3,000 in fines. With few exceptions, however, the players are reluctant to excoriate the refs within range of the media. "You'd have to be crazy to do something like that," says one player. "Because a lot of refs will hold a grudge if you show them up in any way. Darell Garretson is like that. And it's no secret that Sid Borgia always had it in for Rick Barry. Borgia once called three technicals on Barry in about five seconds. Barry could always count on being in foul trouble whenever he played under Borgia's whistle."

The kindest word that most players use to describe NBA officials is "incompetent." The players claim that the officials will either lose control of a ball game or else fight to control it so much that the natural pulse of the game is obliterated. They say there are too many phantom fouls and "ticky-tack" calls. The players also blame the officials for the difficulty that most teams experience in winning on the road. The host team in the NBA has a lifetime winning percentage of 63 percent, and the situation is getting worse. During the '76–'77 season not one ball club played above .500 away from home; Philadelphia came the closest with a record of 18–23. "It's funny," says Phil Jackson, "but I think it's actually easier to get up for a road game. You mostly hang out in a hotel room and you can plan your time pretty much to suit yourself. There are fewer distractions on the road. The players also spend more time together, and that always helps a team play better." Players can't avoid getting tired and jet-lagged, but they all agree that the referees make a big difference. Despite the big-league status of the NBA, most ball clubs have to win at home to draw. It's an old tradition that goes back to the trolley days of the BAA.

Ex-player Archie Clark believes that the refs are also biased along racial lines. "Eighty percent of the protected players are white," says Clark, "even though about two-thirds of the players in the league are black. Most people who pay to see NBA games are white, and they like to identify with their own kind. Black officials have to do what is expected of them if they want to keep their jobs."

The players complain most often about the referees' profound inconsistency. . . . The Knicks are battling the Celtics in Boston, and the score is tied with only ten seconds remaining in the game. The contest has been combative ever since the opening tip-off, and the defensive hand checking has been especially ferocious. Boston has possession and is maneuvering for the winning shot when Jim Cleamons of the Knicks deflects a pass into the backcourt. Boston guard Jo Jo White easily beats Cleamons to the ball: but now there are only three seconds left, and the ball is a harmless 70 feet from the basket. Cleamons is a habitual hustler, and he catches White before the ball is returned across the midcourt stripe. Both players know that the game is bound for overtime, and as White scurries upcourt, Cleamons places a sturdy right hand on Jo Jo's hip to guide him safely toward the buzzer. But the whistle bleats instead, and a foul is called on Cleamons for illegally using his hands on defense. In a flash, White converts two free throws, the Celtics win, and the refs dash off the court. But Cleamons refuses to believe that the game is really over. He hops, stomps, and jumps and tries to articulate his frustration. "What?" he shrieks. "What?" Cleamons finally crouches in despair in front of the Knicks' bench and slams his hands against the floor until a teammate leads him off the floor.

"The refs can drive you nuts," says a veteran player. "If something is always a foul or never a foul, then we can adjust the way we play. But the way things are, you can never tell what they're going to call or when they're going to call it. It's like you're out there playing the game, and then suddenly they yank the floorboards right out from under you."

The league's coaches are likewise distressed at the uneven quality of justice in the NBA. "There are several excellent officials in the league," says Dick Motta, the diminutive coach of the Washington Bullets. "But the pace today is too fast for even two perfect officials to work a good game. Most of the officials are simply out of shape, and most of them are too short. There's only one or two who are over six feet. How can they possibly see around a guy as wide as Darryl Dawkins? They can't get good angles on a play so they have to guess."

Mendy Rudolph has traded his striped shirt for a leisure suit and his whistle for a microphone. Rudolph vehemently denies that the NBA refs practice any kind of favoritism. "There's no such thing as a home-court advantage as far as the refs are concerned," says Rudolph. "Players simply play better at home. With more discernible emotion. And I don't care what anybody says, every player plays under the same rules. A foul is a foul, and a walk is a walk. It's the media that makes the refs look bad. The TV announcers. Turn the sound off, and watch a game. Then you'll see how consistent the officiating really is. People just overreact. In any given game there may be two or three controversial calls that could have gone either way, and in the minds of the fans, the coaches, and the players, the entire game takes on a disputable tone. The official has to call what he sees. It's all a matter of judgment."

It's the opinion of John Nucatola, onetime supervisor of NBA refs, that "basketball officials have the judgment of Supreme Court justices." While on a dead run, an NBA ref must instantly recognize and adjudicate personal fouls, technical fouls, palming transgressions, traveling infractions, goaltending, time-in and -out, and questions of possession and boundary. He must also vibrate at appropriate intervals to detect 3-, 5-, 10-, and 24-second violations. For his troubles, the base salary of a full-time NBA ref ranges from $20,000 to $46,000 for a regular season's schedule of 82 ball games. Preseason games are worked gratis, and the league's senior officials can also earn "overtime" by working play-off games. In addition, the NBA picks up all travel expenses and allots each man $700 a month for seven months to cover hotels, meals, and other incidentals. By virtue of the league rules, NBA refs must travel alone and are prohibited from staying in any hotel already housing one of the ball clubs. In most NBA arenas, the officials' dressing room is protected by an armed guard. Officiating a professional basketball game is a lonely task that borders on the impossible, but for reasons of economy the NBA was hesitant to provide relief.

Every other major sport has taken measures to keep up with today's bigger and faster athletes. Baseball went from three umpires to four in the 1940s, and play-off games, All-Star games, and the World Series now use six men to cover the field of play. Professional football started with three officials and has, through the years, increased that number to seven. Even the National Hockey League, long a bastion of fiscal conservatism, has added a linesman. There's no doubt that NBA officials cover more ground than any of their compatriots. If an average NBA ref blows his whistle sixty times a game, five or six penalties make for a very closely officiated hockey game. Similarly, a football back judge who makes two pass-interference calls in one ball game has seriously tilted the outcome. The only man who approximates the pressure borne by a workaday NBA ref is a home-plate umpire. But an ump can hump up for a play because baseball is played in easily anticipated spurts. And a home-plate umpire assumes the proper position only once every four days. Despite the advent of the 24-second clock, the NBA was reluctant to add officiating personnel.

The NBA first experimented with three game officials during the exhibition seasons of 1971 and 1972, and the advantages of triangulating the game thrilled the players, the coaches, and the referees. "In the games I worked," says Mendy Rudolph, "we didn't miss a call. We had every single play covered. Having a third official adds years to a man's career, and it only takes ten minutes to learn the new positioning." The proposal to add another referee was under discussion by the NBA's Board of Governors for years without ever coming up for a vote. In February of 1978, when the NBA once again tabled the issue, the players demonstrated their displeasure by withdrawing from the league's joint committee on violence. "The procrastination of the NBA is disgraceful," said Larry Fleisher, general counsel of the National Basketball Players' Association. "Their failure to approve a third official is nothing more than a shabby attempt to save money." The total cost of the venture amounts to $28,000 per team—a piddling expenditure considering the perils of perpetuating the status quo. The owners also feared that another official would only slow down the game by calling more fouls and more violations, but Mendy Rudolph was a witness to the contrary. "We actually made fewer calls," says Rudolph. "It was beautiful. You didn't even know we were out there."

The NBA finally added a third official in '78–'79, but only in an attempt to control the on-court violence. Yet even with the added pair of eyeballs, all NBA refs are still forced to accommodate the rule book to suit the rapid-fire realities of the game. "In actual practice," says a veteran NBA official, "we try to judge whether a player gains an advantage by doing certain illegal things. If he walks and doesn't gain anything, we might not call it." So Earl Monroe was allowed to carry the ball whenever he changed direction, and "palming" became a socially acceptable violation. And John Havlicek rarely took a hook shot without first slamming his elbow into somebody's chest. Wilt Chamberlain's "Finger Roll" was always preceded by a shoulder in the face, yet he averaged 45.9 minutes a game for fourteen years without ever fouling out. Players like Chet Walker and Jim Barnett pioneered an illegal "skating" move that's still in vogue. . . . David Thompson of the Denver Nuggets is under tight defensive pressure from Portland's Bobby Gross as he holds the ball at the top of the key. Thompson fakes a shot; then he slides his left foot along the ground for a quick 6 inches. Gross shifts his weight to head off Thompson's apparent thrust to the basket. But then Thompson takes off with a right-foot lead, and Gross is left in the dust.

When Dave Cowens first came into the league in 1970, the officials didn't know him or the physical type of game he had to play to survive, so they penalized him just about every time he touched another player. Cowens led the league with 350 personal fouls during his rookie season, and he finished with fifteen disqualifications. After the officials saw that Cowens was expected to play at least forty to forty-five minutes every game, they gradually gave him more leeway. Conversely, players like Mel Counts and Phil Jackson were always part-timers and always in foul trouble throughout their careers. Sometimes it takes a while for officials to determine what tools a player needs to earn a living in the NBA. "It took four years before the refs let me have my pet move," says Chet Walker. "And I had to do plenty of squawking to get it." But the refs are not always so amenable to every player's style. . . . The Knicks are in a full-court press, spearheaded by the gangling grace of Phil

Jackson. Jackson and a teammate successfully double-team the ball along the sideline. Jackson jabs a snake arm into the melee and pokes the ball loose. But the whistle blows, and Jackson gets tagged with a foul. . . . "It's ridiculous," says Jim McMillian. "The refs just won't let Phil reach for the ball. He's been in the league for ten years, and most of the refs still treat him like a rookie." Sometimes the officials will refuse to "learn" a player's moves. Dave Lattin was a highly touted draft choice of the San Francisco Warriors in 1967, having led Texas Western to the NCAA championship the year before. But the NBA officials decided that Lattin was too aggressive going to the offensive boards, and they simply whistled him right out of the league.

Veteran officials are usually adaptable enough to cope with an impossible situation, but an official can sometimes become too rigid and refuse to accept the unexpected: Big men are not permitted any fancy dribbling, while guards can't get unduly physical. "The refs in the NBA anticipate instead of react," says Calvin Murphy of the Houston Rockets. "They have their minds fixed on what a player's capabilities are. If I block a shot, they automatically call it goaltending because they say to themselves, 'If this guy is only five-nine, he has no business blocking a shot. He must have goaltended.' I also brought a lot of offensive moves with me into the league. But the refs weren't ready for them. They figured I had gotten by my man so easily that I must have taken an extra step."

Everybody agrees that the officiating situation is critical and that a third official will help maintain the stability of the game. There has also been a chorus of other suggestions: Some radical observers propose that a stationary official be seated on a raised chair at midcourt to call zone defenses, goaltendings, and time violations. This would free the on-court refs to concentrate entirely on the development of the ball game. The NBA's coaches suggest that their ranks contain "some of the finest minds in basketball" and that they have nothing but constructive criticism to offer. The coaches would like to see the refs sit in their dressing rooms for half an hour before each game and discuss the task at hand. Because the styles and personnel of every team in the league is unique, each match-up of teams should produce a different tempo. The coaches watch game films and are sensitive to these differences; they feel the officials should respond as well. Several NBA players would require the refs to play the game actively: maybe a weekly full-court run in the playground or perhaps some three-man ball at the Y. Even shooting hoops in a driveway would help keep a referee in touch with the game. The officials themselves believe that higher salaries would attract more and better qualified young men. "One of the biggest problems," says Mendy Rudolph, "is that there are no suitable training grounds for young officials. The NBA uses minor leagues and summer leagues, but they're both inadequate. College games are not much help either. Most college refs would need roller skates to keep up with a pro game."

All parties concur that the NBA should actively recruit voluntarily and involuntarily retired ballplayers. Clyde Lovellette was a 6'9", 280-pounder out of Terre Haute, Indiana, who succeeded George Mikan as the Big Man of the Minneapolis Lakers. Lovellette was a whale near the basket, and he was also a superb outside shooter. His eleven-year career yielded 17.0 points a game with a single season's high of 23.4 in '57–'58. When Lovellette retired in 1964, he was already a hopeless basketball junkie. For the next five years Lovellette aspired to reenter the NBA as an official, but he could never pass the final performance test. Despite his failure, however, Lovellette did get to fulfill the secret fantasy of every NBA official. Upon his final retirement, Lovellette returned to his hometown and became a gun-toting sheriff.

The only ex-player ever accepted into the NBA's officiating fraternity began his journey in 1972 as a lowly seventh-round draft choice of the Phoenix Suns: Bernie Fryer was a sturdy 6'3" guard from Brigham Young University and one of the highest scorers in the school's history. But a bare month after being drafted, Fryer received a telegram from Jerry Colangelo, the general manager of the Suns. Phoenix's roster was already packed with no-cut contracts, and Fryer was notified that the ball club was bringing only its number-one pick (Mike Bantom) to training camp that year. Fryer swallowed his disappointment, got a job, and played some AAU ball back home in Seattle. He was eventually scouted by the Portland Trail Blazers and finally invited to an NBA training camp the following summer. Fryer was always a physical type, with a marked preference for playing rugged defense. At the time the Blazers' offense revolved around the various talents of Sidney Wicks and Geoff Petrie. Fryer was quick to read the situation, and he willingly sacrificed his own offense to point the ball at Wicks and Petrie. Fryer's savvy, guts, and hustle soon elevated him to the third guard slot behind Petrie and Larry Steele. During the '73–'74 season Fryer averaged 20 minutes and 7.0 points for 80 ball games, and he shot .793 from the foul line. He received substantial support in the balloting for the NBA's All-Rookie team, and his future with the Blazers certainly looked secure. Then, just prior to the '74–'75 season, Portland replaced coach Jack McClosky with Lenny Wilkens, a side-winding left-hander who had ostensibly terminated his playing career several months earlier. One of Wilkens's first public announcements stated that he was counting on Fryer to be the Blazers' "playmaking guard." But then, a week before the season commenced, Wilkens reactivated himself as a player and tossed Fryer onto the waiver pile.

Fryer cast around for a few days and then signed on with the St. Louis Spirits of the ABA, a ball club which featured the disembodied adventures of Marvin Barnes: aggravated assault, spontaneous disappearances, rampant egotism, and eventually a six-month stretch in prison. "The ball club was a zoo," says Fryer. "I couldn't stand it. I left after a month, and I finished up the season with the New Orleans Jazz." The '74–'75 Jazz was an expansion club; it had three different head coaches during the first seventeen games of the season (Scotty Robertson, Elgin Baylor, and Butch van Breda Kolff). A total of twenty-two different players appeared on the team's roster, and the anxiety level was so high that the fabulous Pistol Pete Maravich could manage only 21.5 points a game. "It was another zoo," says Fryer. "It made me think twice about the drudgery, the traveling, and the quarreling. I believe I could have played in the NBA for another eight to ten years, but it just wasn't worth it anymore."

At the end of the '74–'75 season Fryer redirected his energies toward becoming a pro official. "I spent a lot of time sitting on the bench with the Jazz," says Fryer, "and I got a chance to watch the officials very carefully. It seemed to be an interesting job. I'd always reffed in city leagues in Seattle just to help out, and I thought I had a certain knack. I sent in an application to the NBA, and I was invited to attend the officials' rookie camp in the summer of 1976."

Don Nelson was another hopeful at the camp, a freshly retired veteran of fourteen illustrious seasons with the Bulls, the Lakers, and the Celtics. "But Don couldn't ref a lick," says Fryer. "He didn't know how to blow the whistle. He didn't know how to hold it. He tried to talk and officiate at the same time. He just didn't look like a ref. But I discovered that I could do a pretty good job myself. I had never reffed in either college or high school, and I had learned the pro game from the start. I passed all the tests, and they seemed to be pleased with my work. Unfortunately they called to offer me a job during the NBA officials' strike of 1976. I hated to be put in that kind of situation, but I was told that this would be the only chance I would ever have to break into the league."

Fryer is firmly convinced that his experience as a player has been a boon. "Most refs coming from college," says Fryer, "or wherever it is that refs come from, are awestruck by the things they see in an NBA ball game. They're not comfortable with the fact that so much of the game is played above the rim, so they call too many goaltendings. They see some of the players making incredible moves, and they say, 'That's impossible. That can't be done legally.' So they blow their whistles too much. I also had the distinct advantage of understanding the players' inner feelings and frustrations. And I also knew many of the players on a first-name basis. It usually takes a ref two or three years to develop that kind of working relationship with the players. Sure, the players beg and cry to me, too, just like they do to all the other refs. But I had an easier time listening to them on a one-to-one basis. Being a ref is a heck of a challenge, and it's the toughest thing I've ever done in my life. But I love it because it keeps me in touch with the soul of the game."

Many of the current ballplayers actually fail to remember Fryer as a player, but the entire league has a growing respect for him as a referee. "Fryer is young," says one player, "so he makes his share of mistakes. Sometimes he goes along with the emotion of a crowd, and he has a tendency to be a homer. I've also seen a lot of players intimidate him. But I think he shows a tremendous amount of potential. Anybody who can make it into the league as a player certainly has all the tools to be a good ref. The same is true of an athlete who's good enough to play topflight college ball. Fryer runs well, and he can keep up with a ball game. He's also alive to the flow of a game. That's his biggest plus. He gets better every time I see him. I'd like to see some other players make the same transition."

As much as players-cum-officials would help preserve the integrity of the game, there's little chance that Fryer's example will ever be duplicated. "Are you kidding me?" asks another player. "I wouldn't be a ref for a million dollars. Those guys are hot dogs. Egomaniacs. Chumps. I didn't know that Fryer used to be a player. But I do know that you'll never see a black ballplayer become a pro official. It's not worth the embarrassment."

4
PITY THE POOR COACH

The '77–'78 preseason edition of the Boston Celtics is being put through the rigors of training camp. The team is headed for a disastrous season with numerous personnel upheavals and will finish out of the play-offs for the first time since Dave Cowens was a rookie. Assistant coach Tom Sanders mans the whistle, and the Celtics run through a defensive shuffle. Head coach Tom Heinsohn rides herd on the rookies, and neither man sees Charlie Scott laughing and dancing through the drill. But the Celtics have a thousand eyes: The practice session is being graced by the august presence of Red Auerbach. Red is immaculately tailored in a cream-colored turtleneck sweater and a brown corduroy jacket. He points a lit cigar at Scott as the players move past the bench. "You loafer," Red hisses. "If it was me, I'd bust your hump." Scott merely laughs and bounces away.

Auerbach exhales a cloud of smoke and rubs his eyes with his knuckles. "Things were sure different when I was coaching," he says. "If I so much as saw a player eating too much, I'd get right on his case. I'd run him when he wanted to rest. I'd make him guard Havlicek in practice. If a guy loafed, I'd send him home and bring in somebody else. Nobody ever heard of a no-cut contract back then. A guy like Don Nelson had five kids. If we didn't get a championship play-off share, Nelson had to get a job for the summer just to keep up. It was much easier being a dictator in those days, and discipline was always my byword. There were no shirttails, no chairs, and no water allowed in practice. I demanded respect. Bob Brannum played for me in the early fifties, and he's about fifty-three now. But when I walked over to Brannum at a party recently, he still hid his drink behind his back. It's a whole new ball game these days. You have to pacify today's players and convince them that what you want them to do is for their own good. These guys don't want to play. The no-cut contract has destroyed incentive. Today's players aren't hungry. It seems that you can't control them, no matter what you do."

Other coaches charge that the average NBA player is functionally uncoachable. They estimate that one-third of the players lack both technique and finesse and are surviving on unadulterated talent. "They look you dead in the eye," says a well-traveled NBA coach. "They nod their heads and say, 'Yeah, yeah, I understand.' Then they go out on the court and do whatever the hell they want." The average NBA athlete is simply too gifted to be objective about his own weaknesses, and he would much rather believe his agent's compliments than his coach's criticism.

If he gets little cooperation from the ball players, an NBA coach usually gets even less assistance from management. The official viewpoint of the corporate franchise owners was best articulated by Gulf and Western's Alan Cohen, the operating head of Madison Square Garden in the early 1970s. "If you ask me whether I'd rather have a basketball championship at the expense of a profit," said Cohen, "I'd have to say no." At the other extreme is the humanistic outlook of Jack Kent Cooke, the "private" owner of the Los Angeles Lakers. "When a man owns a horse that wins the Kentucky Derby," says Cooke, "it's *his* horse. In the same way, the Lakers are *my* team."

Whatever the announced motive, paper profits are never the reason why people are anxious to own an NBA ball club. Over the course of the '73–'74 season, for example, only five of the NBA's twenty-seven franchises made money—New York, Los Angeles, Buffalo, Seattle, and Boston. According to the Internal Revenue Service, the ballplayers currently under contract constitute the bulk of any franchise's value. The true appeal of owning a sports franchise lies in a tax law that allows a team to treat its players' contracts as an asset that gets "used up" over a period of time. An owner can "depreciate" the value of the ballplayers in the same way that he depreciates the typewriter in his secretary's office. The owner can then apply this depreciation against the total profits he makes from all his other business enterprises. If his "NBA deduction" is greater than his other business profits, he pays no taxes at all. A few years ago a group of businessmen purchased an NBA franchise for $3 million. In their first year of operation the new owners actually collected $300,000 more in revenues than they paid out. But when depreciation was figured in, the team was allowed to declare a loss of $1.6 million to the IRS. Each member of the ownership group then subtracted his share of the "loss" and substantially reduced his own taxable income.

There are times, however, when even a tax shelter is too small to hide the frustrations of owning a losing ball club. Tedd Munchak made his millions selling carpets, and in 1972 he owned the hapless Carolina Cougars, the doormats of the ABA. "If Munchak owned a plantation in Africa and lost money," said Carl Scheer, the team's general manager, "no one would know about it. But when a guy loses money on a professional basketball team, everybody knows it—the other owners, the fans, and his pals at the club. I know the public image of failure has hurt Tedd a great deal."

Other owners are only too anxious to agonize in public when their teams lose. At one time Jack Kent Cooke would express his dissatisfaction by sitting courtside and screaming abuse at any Lakers who made a mistake. Rudy LaRusso played for Los Angeles from 1960 to 1967, and he is still irked at Cooke's tactics. "The whole thing was not conducive to good basketball," says LaRusso. "We got frantic about having to win every game, and we tried to cut things too fine. We were never in a position to just go out and play. There was also a mountain of extra pressure on coach Fred Schaus."

There are only a limited number of devices which an NBA coach can use to try to control his players: fines for carelessness and decreased playing time for stubbornness. But fines are ineffective and, playing time is often regulated by management. Players will bitch about being fined, yet they regret the subsequent razzing of their teammates more than the financial loss. In 1976 Tates Locke became the coach of the Buffalo Braves only upon agreeing that the short, chubby, slow, and defenseless Ernie DiGregorio would play at least thirty minutes a game. In '76–'77 coach Red Holzman received word that Bill Bradley and Phil Jackson were being phased out and were to be used only when another player needed a breather. Holzman forthwith announced his retirement and made his own substitutions for the remainder of the season.

"It's management's job to get the players," says Eddie Donovan, general manager of the Knicks. "It's the coach's job to coach them." So coaches are rarely consulted by management when important personnel decisions are being made. In 1977 the front office of the Chicago Bulls overruled coach Ed Badger and ordered the release of a rookie guard named Mike Glenn, who moved on to Buffalo and became a sharpshooting sensation. During the same season Jack Kent Cooke presented his latest coach, Jerry West, with a surprise package: Ernie DiGregorio and a fat no-cut pact. West complained so bitterly that Cooke ate part of the contract and DiGregorio was released in midseason. . . . "Owners are overly influenced by personality factors," says Dean Meminger, a six-year player with Atlanta and New York. "Owners are concerned with trivial things like ego power and statistics. They have no idea what the game is really about. But they think they know more than anybody. These are the guys who are tying the hands of the coaches and turning the NBA into a stupid league."

As soon as the courts killed the option clause and declared that pro athletes were free agents when their contracts expired, a new philosophy took hold of professional sports. The owners became convinced that the only way to win championships was to collect expensive talent and man every position with a superstar. George Steinbrenner's famous free-agent orgies brought the New York Yankees Jim ("Catfish") Hunter, Don Gullett, Reggie Jackson, Rich Gossage, and World Series titles in 1977 and 1978. But the persistent failures of the New York Knicks, the Los Angeles Lakers, and the Philadelphia 76ers show that in professional basketball the whole team concept is still greater than the sum of the parts.

In addition to a coach's other problems, the hectic NBA schedule limits his opportunities to do any serious coaching. Training camp is used almost exclusively to scrutinize new players and to get everybody into playing shape. The season extends from October to May (and sometimes even into June), and a team will often play 4 games in five nights in four different cities—games that are physical to the point of brutality. By Thanksgiving literally every player in the league is nursing at least one nagging injury. By Christmas a coach is fortunate to be able to summon eight bodies for practice. To make matters worse, the owners will often infringe on those valuable early-season practices when all the players are healthy. . . . It's 10:00 a.m. on a Saturday just two weeks into the '72–'73 NBA season. Last night the Baltimore Bullets defeated the Knicks in a tense ball game, and the Bullets are in a good mood as they prepare to face Wilt Chamberlain and the Lakers at home on Sunday afternoon. The time is perfect for a spirited, productive practice session. Instead, the team has driven forty-five minutes through a light rain to a junior high school gymnasium, where one thousand screaming kids have paid out a thousand wrappers from Mars candy bars for the privilege of witnessing a "Baltimore Bullets Basketball Clinic."
While the urchins fidget in the stands and the ballplayers

squirm on the bench, a matron in a red pants suit welcomes everybody to Silver Spring, Maryland. There are rumors that the Baltimore franchise will soon be relocated somewhere in the area. Perhaps to nearby Landover. "Before we meet the Bullets," says the hostess, "let me tell all of you girls and boys about something that's really important."

Stan Love, the Bullets' resident flake, widens his eyes.

"Mars candy," says the red pants suit, "has come up with a wonderful new treat I'm sure you'll all enjoy. It's called Munch Peanut Brittle. Tell your mommies and daddies to go to the store and get some."

Stan Love pretends to retch inside his jersey. "I always get nervous before clinics," he explains.

The clinic gets under way with a question-and-answer period, and the first query comes from a cub scout: "Is it true that Mike Riordan has a map of Ireland tattooed on his belly?"

"No," says coach Gene Shue, the stern-faced quizmaster.

"It's on his face," says Love.

Next question: "What kind of girls does Elvin Hayes like?"

"His wife," says Shue.

"End of question-and-answer period," says Elvin Hayes.

The Big E grabs a basketball, trots onto the court, and begins shooting lay-ups. His teammates quickly join him. After a few minutes the Bullets break into a scrimmage: Passes are thrown into the stands, shots are thrown from the hip, and candy wrappers are thrown on the floor. Coach Shue mutters an occasional "Nice defense" and checks his watch every five minutes. After a decent interval Shue nods to Hayes, and the Bullets speed out a side door and head for the dressing room. Grandma Munch comes running over to Shue. "But the clinic, the clinic," she pleads.

"You just saw it," Shue says over his shoulder.

The players face cold showers, no soap, a shortage of towels, and a $25 gratuity from Abe Pollin, their grateful owner. Gene Shue faces a breach of team harmony, a wasted chance to get something accomplished, and a certain loss on Sunday.

"Management is always interfering with a coach's ability to do a good job," says Al Attles, coach and GM of the Golden State Warriors. "In Philadelphia the owners want Julius Erving to score and put on a show. They know that people like to see a guy get a bundle of points. They also know that the majority of the fans want to see spectacular plays more than they want to see good team basketball. But this kind of thinking means that somebody has to be forcing a lot of shots when his teammates are wide open. If you want to coach in the NBA and keep your sanity, then you have to make excuses to yourself."

Some coaches try to relieve the pressure by preaching the game to Xs and Os behind closed doors in darkened rooms, by spending lonely slow-motion hours with a finger on the magic button and moving flickering images back and forth through time. . . . When Milwaukee coach Larry Costello was asked, "What happened?" after a play-off loss a few years ago, he said flatly, "I can't make any comments until I see the game films."

As offenses and defenses become more intricate, NBA coaches are obliged to spend more time studying game films. This necessity has become universal in the NBA, especially with the recent influx of college coaches (Bill Fitch, Jack Ramsay, Tom Nissalke, Dick Motta, Jack McCloskey, Bill van Breda Kolff, Herb Brown, Tates Locke, John MacLeod, Dick Vitale, and Ed Badger), who learned their techniques in a frantic 30-game season. Even Tom ("Satch") Sanders coached at Harvard for four years before becoming Tommy Heinsohn's assistant (and successor) with the Boston Celtics in 1977. Sanders is a long-legged, short-waisted, and infinitely dignified graduate of New York University, and a Celtic for thirteen seasons and eight championships. "The proper use of game films is a science and an art," says Sanders. "I spend entire summers watching hundreds of ball games, then editing and splicing them into categories. The Celtics have two reels of out-of-bounds plays, several reels of fast breaks, ·set plays, defenses, jump balls. . . . Everything. We use these films as teaching devices. When the Celtics show movies in summer camp, pads and pencils are distributed, and even the veterans are expected to take notes. Game films are also useful in scouting opponents and evaluating talent. Unfortunately some coaches get carried away with a good thing." . . . One veteran NBA coach frequently astounds his players by showing game films at halftime. The coach replays the last few minutes of the recently concluded half and conducts a windy soliloquy. "It's ludicrous," says one player. "There we are, all sweaty, competitive, and in the middle of a ball game. Watching the films only makes us drowsy."

Some coaches are power brokers who tell their players what to wear, where to eat, and what to drive. Bill Russell is unanimously alleged to have been the worst offender. Other coaches are milksops. When Roy Rubin left Long Island University to coach the Philadelphia 76ers in 1972, his first official act was to convene his new team and lay down the law. "Under no conditions will I tolerate smoking in the locker room," Rubin insisted. "There will be no exceptions to this rule."

One of the ballplayers, Fred ("Mad Dog") Carter, was devastated by the news. "But, coach," said Carter, "I can't hit a shot in the second half unless I smoke my cigarette at halftime. I've been smoking ever since I've been in the league." Rubin cogitated as Carter's teammates nodded their assent. "All right," Rubin finally said. "Let's try this. . . . Nobody is allowed to smoke in the locker room except for you."

The entire team was instantly sprawled on the floor with laughter, and Rubin's fate was sealed. Rubin lasted only 51 games, and he left the NBA with a lifetime record of 4–47.

If some coaches are intimidated by their players, there are also some who hate them. "My players are stupid and arrogant beyond belief," says a well-traveled NBA coach. "They come to practice with their hair in braids and wearing ridiculous hats. Then they refuse to break an honest sweat. They have no respect for anything but their own welfare. They don't want to be shown anything new. I tried to reach them, but after a while I just said the hell with them. Now I just throw out the ball and let them make fools of themselves. We have a winning record, but any smart team can take us apart."

Some of "the finest minds in basketball" are also jokesters, politicians, con men, madmen, teachers, students, geniuses, and incompetents. The only successful coaches are the ones who can first find a way to get along with the players and then compel them to believe in the game instead of themselves. Al Attles, Jack Ramsay, Larry Brown, John MacLeod, Kevin Loughery, Tom Heinsohn, and Hubie Brown are generally considered to be the league's premier coaches. But even a great coach is always at the mercy of his situation.

"I think it's already too late to save the game," says Steve Kuberski, a nine-year man with Boston, Milwaukee, and Buffalo. "The coaches are powerless, the owners are crazy, and even the ballplayers are unhappy. Salaries, rents, and ticket prices all keep climbing. Unless something drastic happens, I don't think the NBA can last another ten years. Professional basketball will probably have to go international to survive." Lest Kuberski be deemed an irresponsible alarmist, his dire warning is echoed by several other players. "Ten years, hell," says an NBA veteran. "Somewhere, sometime, there's going to be another vicious punch-out like Kermit Washington and Rudy Tomjanovich. . . . Or else a really emotional coach will freak out over a bad call. . . . And there'll be a full-scale riot. There's an awful lot of personal tension, competitive tension, and racial tension in the NBA. Everybody's frustration level is very high, including the fans'. I think the league is lucky if it lasts until 1984."

The NBA's problems may be ticking loudly, and the final buzzer may be nigh. . . . But have no fear. The solutions are already at hand. And Basketball Jones lives.

5

BASKETBALL JONES LIVES!

Basketball Jones lives in Harlem, U.S.A. Some say he was born at centercourt in the Holcombe Rucker Memorial Playground on 155th Street and Eighth Avenue. . . .

It's a blustery autumnal morning, a Tuesday, and the welfare eagle will fly as soon as the mailman comes. Meanwhile, the wind sweeps through the park, stirring the dead leaves and the half-dead winos and undressing yesterday's newspapers. A dozen black men lounge along one section of bench. They share a battered copy of the *Daily News,* which they all read from back page to front. They also circulate a bottle of wine and a joint. Their lips dance with laughter, taunts, and schemes while they ask after the time.

The wind slices through the basketball court, shaking the two bent rims and bowing a clump of weeds that sprout through the asphalt along the far base line. A pair of nervous young men prowl one of the baskets and shoot junk shots with a faded ABA ball. At the other basket, six teenagers play hooky and three-on-three. A light-skinned player with a menacing Oriental mustache dribbles at the top of the key. He wears a short-sleeved maroon sweat shirt, cut-off jeans, and Adidas. His defender is taller and warmer in a shabby blue parka. The light-skinned player dribbles furiously in one spot, twitching and feinting until at last his opponent tilts to his toes. Then a sharp spin to the right, a high-flying jump shot that clangs against the backboard and springs off the front rim. There's never any "retrieving" in Harlem, so the errant shot transforms all six players into offensive rebounders. The light-skinned youth snatches the ball and uncorks a fadeaway jumper. "In your face," he says, but the shot misses. Then a blue parka bounds from the pack and taps the ball through the hoop before it lands. It's winners' out, and the ball game continues.

Suddenly a fire engine screams down Eighth Avenue. The men on the benches crane their necks. The junkies try to hide in each other's shadows. But the basketball players know that turned heads allow easy lay-ups, and the game goes on.

"Hey, man! It's a fire!" yells one of the men. "Look! You can see the smoke!"

But the ballplayers persevere.

"Check this out," the man says to his benchmates, giggling. Then he turns to the basketball court and cups his hands around his mouth. "Hey, Chink!" he shouts. "Ain't that your house burnin', man?"

"Yeah, Chink!" chimes another man. "Your house is on fire!"

The ball game stops. Chink has just missed another jump shot. "Yeah," he snarls. "Fuck it. Ain't nobody home anyway. . . . It's my ball, man. That dude was yellin' at me while I was shootin'. That's offensive interference."

The men on the bench quake with laughter, and even the junkies smile. "You hear that shit?" one of the addicts whispers.

"Yeah," clucks the other as he scratches his veins. "That poor nigger. He got the worst Jones I ever saw."

Basketball Jones lives in Atlanta, where coach Hubie Brown runs the Hawks through an early-season practice session at the Omni.

Brown is 6' tall, but thin and slightly stooped. Only his ruddy face and sparkling hazel eyes belie his forty-six years. He runs the Hawks undefensed through the offensive plays for twenty-five minutes. The players are bored, but Brown drives them until their choreography and timing are meticulous. Then, suddenly, a forward deviates from his proscribed path and lofts in a 25-foot jumper. "Great shot, baby," Brown shouts with a lopsided grin. "But, hey . . . that ain't the play."

"I scored, didn't I?" The player smiles.

Brown is instantly whipped into a mild froth. "Listen up," he tells the group. "One guy breaks the pattern, scores, and the fans go bullshit, and his girlfriend shrieks 'My hero!' But what happens when the next guy misses, and we're out of our offense and getting our butts kicked by 25 points? So don't give me that bullshit—'the shot went in.' I'm telling you, if you don't take the kind of shot that helps the ball club, you're gonna be gone."

Brown next breaks the team into a scrimmage. He stands imperiously at midcourt, hawking the action and prodding the players. "Get your ass in gear, or get the hell out of the gym," he yells at one player. "Don't worry about the mistake," he shouts to another. "You hustled, and that's all I can ask." When Eddie Johnson, a rookie guard from Auburn, sets a woeful offensive screen, Brown stops play. "That's not a screen," says Brown. "That's a beauty pose. You have to get the position, Eddie. Then stand strong, take the punishment, and create a one-step advantage for your teammate. And, hey . . . you help him, Eddie, and he'll help you."

Hubie Brown is abrasive, blunt, self-righteous, knowledgeable, compassionate, and courageous. The Hawks' owner is Ted Turner—a world-champion yachtsman, owner of the Atlanta Braves, and compleat millionaire—whose temperament matches Brown's stride for stride. In their own crazy fashion, Brown and Turner are getting back to basics and returning a semblance of sanity to the NBA. Their '77–'78 Atlanta Hawks stunned the basketball community by playing .500 ball and gaining the play-offs with a low-talented "economy" roster.

John Drew, Tom McMillen, and Wayne Rollins have the only no-cut contracts on the team, and the average player salary is $77,000, or half the league average.

"Most of my guys barely make the league minimum of thirty thousand dollars," boasts Brown. "They're castoffs. But they're hungry and coachable. They're willing to put their guts on the line for forty-eight minutes a game because they want to prove they can compete in the NBA. I'm committed to the team concept. I play ten men every quarter to give everybody a chance to contribute. I also believe in the wagon-train philosophy. Back then you didn't get paid if you didn't put in an honest day's work. It's the same way around here. I read them the waiver lists every week to remind them of how many other guys want their jobs."

Brown has Turner's enthusiastic support, and the Hawks scan the collegiate draft with a frugal eye. In 1977 the Hawks' number-one pick was Wayne Rollins, a promising 7'1" shot blocker and rebounder, who averaged a mere 14.1 points a game during his senior year at Clemson. Rollins was flattered to be the fourteenth player selected in the entire draft, and he was glad to sign a one-year no-cut contract at a bargain price of $80,000. One can only ponder the size of the contracts offered to the Hawks' other priority draft picks: Dave Bormann of Gardner-Webb, Bill Gorden of Tennessee (Chattanooga), Calvin Crews of S.W. Louisiana, and James Holiman of Arizona State. Rollins was the only "big-name" draftee to make the team, but Hubie Brown found 5'8" Charlie Criss in the Eastern League and turned him into a very grateful twenty-nine-year-old NBA rookie.

Most owners believe they must draft college superstars—i.e., scorers— in order to satisfy the fans' expectations. It's true that almost 90 percent of the players in the NBA were either first-, second-, or third-round draft choices. But there are always an abundance of hardworking, highly skilled college players who don't even rate headlines in their own school newspaper. Tom

Abernethy was the unsung hero of Indiana University's 1976 NCAA champs and a far better player than either of his All-American teammates Kent Benson or Scott May. Don Adams and Jim Fox were both humble number-eight picks who enjoyed long and productive careers in the NBA. Bob Dandridge and M. L. Carr were number-four selections, Steve Mix was number five, and All-Star guard Randy Smith began his pro career as a lowly number-seven pick. Since they were chosen primarily to fill up the training-camp rosters, the success of most of these players was "accidental." The Atlanta Hawks, on the other hand, are systematically disregarding college statistics and drafting instead for character and compatibility.

"I want ballplayers who are willing to sacrifice," says Hubie Brown. "I want complete ballplayers who are willing to accept a specific role and a specific set of responsibilities. There's one quotation from Calvin Coolidge I've been using for years: 'There's nothing more common than unsuccessful people with great potential.' Our goal at Atlanta is to become successful by finding players who will at least play up to their potential all the time. And we think we've already succeeded. If nothing else, whenever anyone talks about basketball's miracle teams, the '77–'78 Atlanta Hawks will be remembered."

Basketball Jones lives in Portland. . . . In 1974, when Lenny Wilkens replaced Jack McCloskey as coach of the Trail Blazers, he inherited a discontented, uncongenial ball club. Geoff Petrie and Sidney Wicks dominated the team—both of them volatile scorers and antagonistic personalities. Wicks was a UCLA grad and a veteran of three NCAA championship teams in the "Lew Alcindor" era. As a pro Wicks played on only one winning ball club during his first seven seasons in the NBA, and his points per game average relentlessly declined in each of those years. Wicks had a textbook case of "superstaritis," but he also had such an abundance of talent that he played in four All-Star games. Petrie was a Princeton man and an offensive machine.

At center for the Trail Blazers was Bill Walton, a celebrated rookie from UCLA. Walton had powered his alma mater to NCAA titles in 1972 and 1973, and the Bruins lost a total of only 4 games during that span. The media touted Walton as an "instant savior," and the Portland fans welcomed him into their hearts. But then Walton showed up with his hair in a ponytail, and the town was aghast. Walton immediately began to complain about the weather and espouse radical political causes.

Despite their sympathetic background, there was no chance that Wicks and Walton could ever play together in harmony. "Guys from UCLA tend to be paranoid," observes an NBA veteran. "John Wooden was a very powerful man, and his players aren't used to losing. Pros from UCLA are famous for being critical and intolerant of their teammates. Walton wasn't really so bad. He was just young and susceptible to bad advice. But Sidney could bitch enough for both of them." The hostility finally brimmed over one day in practice when Wicks tried to decapitate Walton with a full-court pass thrown from five feet away.

The turmoil was more than Walton could handle, and the rookie soon began breaking down with a variety of injuries. He played in only 35 ball games, and the Trail Blazers finished 6 games under .500 and out of the play-offs. Then, through a Los Angeles connection, word leaked out that Walton's infirmities were make-believe and that he wanted out of Portland. The outraged Portland fans began wearing WALTON GO HOME buttons.

The only meaningful roster change made for the following season was the addition of two topnotch rookies: Lionel Hollins, a 6′4″ guard from Arizona State, and Bob Gross, a 6′5″ forward from Long Beach State. Wilkens also retired for good; but the basic team chemistry remained the same, and the '75–'76 season was a replica of the previous one: Wicks and Petrie were the high scorers, and the team continued to blaze with dissension. Walton was subject to another rash of injuries and appeared in only 51 ball games. The team wound up 8 games under .500 and at the bottom of their division. Then, in the spring of 1976, the unfortunate Wilkens was fired, and Jack Ramsay was lured from Buffalo to succeed him.

Jack Ramsay has been coaching in the NBA since 1968. Before that, he coached for eleven years at St. Joseph's College in Philadelphia where he was widely renowned as a wizard of the zone defense. Before that, Ramsay was a minor-league basketball player, whom contemporaries still describe as "one of the dirtiest players who ever lived." Ramsay is fiftyish nowadays, but he is still tall, trim, and limber. He is forceful in a quiet way, and even his wrinkles radiate health and conviction. Ramsay is, in fact, a health-food enthusiast who leads the team through their daily calisthenics. Above all else, Ramsay is a rational man, and he understood that Bill Walton was the kind of player seen only once in a generation. Ramsay was empowered by owner Lawrence Weinberg to adjust the ball club to fit the big man's capabilities, and he wasted no time. Lionel Hollins and Bob Gross were eager, adroit, and malleable. Larry Steele and Lloyd Neal were limited but productive. Sidney Wicks was sold outright to Boston. Geoff Petrie was sent to Atlanta, along with reserve center Steve Hawes for the Hawks' selection in the ABA dispersal draft. The Chicago Bulls had the first choice, and they tabbed 7'2" Artis Gilmore. Ramsay was up next, and he picked a 6'8", 240-pound temperamental forward named Maurice Lucas. "I knew Lucas had problems with all his previous coaches," said Ramsay. "But all he asked for was to be treated with respect. That didn't seem like such a hard bargain for me to keep."

Two days before the '76–'77 training camp convened, Lucas arrived in Portland and went out to dinner with Walton. The two young men soon discovered that they were both essentially private individuals with mutual interests in vegetarianism, backpacking, meditation, and communism. Ramsay's gardening bore fruit the very same season: Walton remained brilliantly intact for 65 regular season games. The team exuded goodwill, they all ate yogurt, and the Blazers came from nowhere to rout the mighty Philadelphia 76ers and cop the NBA crown in 1977.

Cynics say that winning is the only thing that begets harmony and that superior talent is the only thing that wins. Yet it's no secret that beyond Walton, Hollins, and Lucas, the 1977 championship Trail Blazers were actually one of the least "talented" teams in the league. "The difference is role playing," says the legendary John Havlicek. "All the Portland players are willing to work hard without the ball. They're not at all concerned with their own statistics or personal accomplishments. Most of the ballplayers in the NBA don't really believe that basketball is a team game and that there's a method to winning. Role playing is almost a lost art these days."

On the surface there are only three positions in basketball: guard, forward, and center. But there are small guards, big guards, penetrating guards, shooting guards, ball-handling guards, and defensive guards. There are centers who face the basket and centers who play with their backs to the hoop. There are small forwards, inside forwards, outside forwards, swing forwards, and power forwards. There's even a backwards-forward. A player's role depends on his size, his abilities, his attitude, and his coach. And the first duty for every basketball coach is to design a system whereby each of his players has a discernible role.

But you don't have to own a pair of sneakers or a can of game films to be One with The Game. All you need is the realization that the traditional means of describing, regulating, and measuring professional basketball are either inadequate or misleading. . . . Then just slow down, lean back, move your attention away from the bouncing ball. . . . And believe that Basketball Jones will catch you should you fall.

6

"WOE UNTO THE WORLD BECAUSE OF OFFENSES!"

A serious basketball game is divided into three elements: offense, defense, and transition—the moments between offense and defense. There are several manners of team offense in the NBA, each having its own purpose and methodology. The fast-break offense gets rolling on the principle that lay-ups are easier to make than jump shots. If the lifetime shooting percentage of the NBA hovers about 46 percent, professional basketball players make only 88 percent of their lay-ups. Easy shots are missed because the shooter relaxes and loses concentration. Easy shots are also missed because they're not so easy. . . . Lionel Hollins has beaten his man and is gliding to the hoop, but Kareem Abdul-Jabbar stalks over from the other side of the basket to menace the shot. Hollins fakes and clutches while at the top of his jump; on his way down, Hollins switches hands, dips under the big man's wingspread, and banks home an "easy lay-up." . . . Running teams are satisfied if they can convert 65 percent of their fast-break opportunities. The Denver Nuggets, San Antonio Spurs, Portland Trail Blazers, and Boston Celtics are fast-breaking teams. Under coach Willis Reed, the New York Knicks unsuccessfully strived to become one.

A fast break always starts with a defensive rebound, so the first priority of a breaking team is to control the boards. Most teams rely on two rebounders (Maurice Lucas and Bill Walton for Portland) and send three men out on the break. Teams with a dominant rebounding center like Bill Russell, Wilt Chamberlain, or Nate Thurmond can release four men downcourt. But the classic fast break remains the three-on-two. . . . Billy Paultz snares a rebound, turns toward the near sideline, and fires a 20-foot line-drive chest pass. Paultz is adept at executing the single most important pass in basketball—the outlet pass. The big man's delivery hits teammate Mike Gale in the hands just as Gale crosses the midcourt line. Gale is the Spurs' best ball handler, and he veers slightly and dribbles closer to the center of the court. Gale is now the triggerman, and he aims the fast break straight at the basket so that both sides of the court are within easy passing range. Running abreast of Gale are the wingmen—guard George Gervin and forward Larry Kenon. Gale reaches the top of the key, and the wingmen continue to hug the sidelines. As soon as Gervin and Kenon approach an imaginary extension of the foul line, they explode to the hoop. The outmanned defensive tandem replies with a one-one stack zone, one man in front of the other. The top man defenses Gale to a halt just above the foul line, and the back man hustles to cover Gale's snappy bounce pass to Gervin. Since Gervin is now under guard, he sails a perfect pass to Kenon, and the fast break is consummated with a dunk shot.

There are several species of fast breaks: The Denver Nuggets and the Phoenix Suns use defensive pressure to coax fast-break opportunities. The San Diego Clippers' running game is headed by the breakaways of Randy Smith; the Boston Celtics like to get 6'5" forward Billy Knight involved near the basket before the big men get back on defense. At one time, the potency of the Philadelphia 76ers' running game came from its versatility: four of Philadelphia's starters (guards Doug Collins and Henry Bibby, as well as forwards George McGinnis and Julius Erving) are good enough ball handlers to trigger the break. And until explosive guard Brian Taylor took a powder midway through the '77–'78 season, the Nuggets also launched a relay of four sprinters on the break—Taylor, Bobby Wilkerson, Bobby Jones, and David Thompson. But the unique fast break in the NBA is perennially demonstrated by the Boston Celtics.

The Celtics feel that a five-on-four advantage is just as effective as any other and is, in fact, the easiest to come by. "The fast break is an attitude," says Tom Heinsohn. "Everybody rebounds, and everybody runs. The idea is to keep constant pressure on the defense and to attack their desire to win. The Celtics want to force the defensive players to think much faster than they are used to thinking. The Celtics also go after a team's physical conditioning, especially the big men. The Celtics want to wear out the big men and catch them loafing by the second quarter. How long is it going to take for the poor suckers who do get back on defense to get pissed at their teammates who aren't hustling? 'Screw you,' they're going to say. 'I quit.' The Celtics want to break down the other team's morale and create dissension."

One refinement of the traditional Celtic fast break often created something even more damaging than dissension. "Dave Cowens used to run downcourt at the tail end of the fast break," says Phil Jackson, "and they timed it so that John Havlicek would cross Cowens's back. If you were guarding Havlicek, it would hit you like a pick on the run from the blind side. All of a sudden you'd go down, and Havlicek had a free lane to the basket. And the officials never called it."

The fast break can also be an entire offense unto itself. If no acceptable shot materializes immediately, the wingmen continue along the base line and exchange sides. This opens lanes for the two trailing big men. If there are still no open shots, most teams will try to exploit any mismatches caused by the initial offensive overload. Even after the defense has fully recovered, there's invariably a guard defending a forward, a forward defending a center, or a center defending nobody. These "situations" can produce relatively easy shots without much further ado.

"When Cowens was a rookie," says Tom Heinsohn, "the only offensive play I taught all year was a five-man, twenty-four-second-long fast break. There was one option for the trigger-man and one each for the wingmen. But everybody just kept flowing through the foul lane, changing sides and setting picks away from the ball. Some of the players made a fuss and accused me of undercoaching. But the fast break is all the offense a team really needs. And it's a mother to play against. The other team gets so apprehensive about getting back on defense that they rush their own offense." Fast-break teams obviously run more than others and can force their opponents into premature exhaustion. "Running teams make the other team play their ninth and tenth men," notes Heinsohn. "This has to reduce their overall effectiveness as a ball club. But running teams have to be deep, too. That's why fast-breaking teams take such a long time to build."

Ball clubs that play pattern offenses can usually get along with only eight seasoned players. A pattern team works the ball much more conservatively than a fast-break team. Ball-control teams require patience, persistence, and an abiding faith in their ability to always find a good shot. "Set plays are designed to create mismatches," says Dave Cowens. "If a player is strong but not quick, then you maneuver him into situations where he has to use quickness. If he's quick but not extensively strong, you want to force him closer to the basket." A deliberate offense will run every defender into three or four picks on every play, make him play defense for a full twenty to twenty-four seconds, and stretch his concentration. If a defender accepts a single pick or turns his head just once to follow the ball, then BANG! . . . The right man has the ball in the right place at the right time, and the offense rings up two easy points.

The Chicago Bulls, New Jersey Nets, Washington Bullets, Los Angeles Lakers, and Phoenix Suns are examples of contemporary teams that depend mostly on set plays to score their points. But the vintage Knicks of the late 1960s were the epitome of a well-balanced ball-control team. . . . Bill Bradley scampered around the court like a mad scientist, his eyes bulging with intensity and each cocked eyebrow pointing in a different direction. . . . Willis Reed ran only as fast as his gimpy knee could take him, but Willis was a rock with sufficient inner resources to intimidate Wilt Chamberlain with a crippled leg in the seventh game of the 1969 championship series. . . . Dave DeBusschere ran when he had to, and he expended most of his basketball energy in pushing his chest into the face of the man he was guarding. . . . Walt Frazier's face was always frozen; but his rhythm was hot, and his hands were greedy for steals and game-winning baskets. . . . Earl Monroe weaved his body through one dimension and the basketball through another. "The Black Jesus" would oftentimes transubstantiate a ball game into a miracle. . . . The Knicks took full advantage of whatever fast breaks were available, but they ran plays 60 percent of the time. Their repertoire included twenty-five to thirty plays, all of them well known to every defense in the league. But the Knicks were geniuses of timing, execution, cooperation, and adjustment, and Red Holzman piloted them to NBA titles in 1969 and 1973. After Reed's knee was finally totaled, the '72–'73 Knicks featured Dave DeBusschere (a forward) and Jerry Lucas (a center) playing out on the offensive perimeter and shooting 30-foot bombs. This tactic astonished the sensibilities of the league's big men and lured them far beyond their normal defensive environment. The Knicks would then complete the switch by having their guards, Frazier and Monroe, back their men into the open middle for short jumpers, "easy lay-ups," or crisp passes to wide-open teammates.

In spite of the Knicks' example, most fast-break coaches think very little of pattern offenses. "Patterns are simply a crutch in place of fast breaks," says Phil Johnson, the coach of the Kansas City Kings from 1973 to 1978. "They are used so that a team can get a good shot every time down the court. Patterns are used to force the ballplayers into doing the things on offense that they should be doing naturally. Things like cutting to the basket and picking away from the ball. Patterns also insure good court balance and prevent point-hungry players from hanging around the basketball. But pattern teams demand great maturity and discipline from the players. They also allow the defense too much time to set up." According to Tommy Heinsohn, pattern offenses also stifle creativity. "Most ballplayers would rather run," says Heinsohn. "And every team has to run to some degree. Today's defenses are so tough that you've got to get as many easy baskets as you can."

There are other teams in the NBA whose offenses may begin with a fast break or a pattern but usually wind down into a one-on-one confrontation. Under laboratory conditions, an NBA player can beat a single defender about 80 percent of the time. Teams like the Philadelphia 76ers and the New Orleans Jazz are offensively interested in isolating superstars on their favorite areas of the court. But no matter how superb the superstar or how attractive the odds, a one-on-one offense is actually the easiest to contain. "The other four guys stand around and watch the guy with the ball," says Phil Jackson. "They become almost useless, and the defense can afford to collapse around the ball without getting burned. The more players a team involves in its offense, the harder the team is to defense."

Every team in the NBA employs a mixture of fast breaks, set plays, and one-on-one situations. But there are two other generic terms used to describe a pro team's offense: "White Basketball" and "Black Basketball." And the difference is real. . . . Dean ("The Dream") Meminger still lives in Harlem. His NBA career is apparently over at age twenty-nine, and Meminger is seriously considering becoming either a TV sports commentator or a law student. Meminger is still lean, bouncy, and fawn-legged, and his face still beams when he speaks. "You've got to kick and scratch to survive in the ghetto," he says. "Nobody does anything for you except to try and rip you off. You learn quickly that you're all alone. And when you play basketball, the same independent attitude that you're forced to develop just carries over onto the court. As you grow up, you also realize it's going to be almost impossible for you to be a doctor or a lawyer. . . . There are very few professional black people in the neighborhood for you to identify with. And it's hard to see how reading about how many bananas South America exports or adding up some numbers is going to help you make it. So you go with what you do best, what you enjoy best, and what you see black men succeeding at best— basketball. It's one of the few legal ways that a black boy can be a man and develop some self-respect. It's a terrible situation, but that's the way it is.

"And then you go to high school or, if you're lucky enough, to college. Then some white basketball coach tells you that you've got to learn to play basketball exactly the way *he* says. And if you have trouble accommodating yourself to him, he says you're copping an attitude. He tells you that the team is more important than you are. . . . And that all five ballplayers have to help each other. Let me ask you, man. How can a kid from the South Bronx or Watts believe all of that? It goes against everything he's ever learned in the streets and the playgrounds. But if you've got a good enough coach and a good enough headset, you learn and you adjust. If you can do it, you learn that working with four other guys makes everything easier for you. You learn that you don't have to work as hard to get the same things done. You also learn to define yourself in a different way. Scoring 30 points a game and losing ain't nothing. . . . Look at Tiny Archibald. He's tired of the superstar trip, and now he wants to win. Believe me, winning is the ultimate trip. . . . Listen, man. The ghetto game is fine for the ghetto, but not for the NBA. In the playground, if a guy makes me look bad, I can come right back and try to do the same to him. In the NBA I had to sublimate my personal game. If Pete Maravich, say, wiped me out and we still won, well . . . That's all the ego satisfaction I needed. But it's very hard for most black ballplayers to make the adjustment. Let's put it in street terms. . . . They don't realize that it's much easier to pick a guy's pocket than to bop him on the head and steal his wallet."

Acceptable behavioral models abound in White America, and most white children enjoy a healthy range of outlets for their growing egos. They play basketball in gleaming gyms instead of rusty schoolyards, and they play under constant supervision and instruction. NBA coaches of all shades agree that white basketball players get consistently superior coaching at every level and imbibe the team concept at an early age. Over the past twenty years there has been a significant shortage of white ballplayers who excelled at one-on-one. Those who do or did include Paul Arizin, George Yardley, Richie Guerin, Billy Cunningham, John Rudometkin, Jerry West, Paul Westphal, Gail Goodrich, and Pete Maravich.

Jackie Robinson broke baseball's "color line" in 1947, and over the next few years other "Negroes" were allowed into the major leagues: Larry Doby, Luke Easter, Dan Bankhead, Don New-combe, Roy Campanella, and Satchel Paige. But the NBL, BAA, and neophyte NBA were all lily-white. In the late 1940s, if a black athlete wanted to turn pro, his only legal choices were baseball, prizefighting, or Abe Saperstein's Harlem Globetrot-ters. Saperstein had a monopoly on the black basketball market, and the Globetrotters have logged well over one hundred million miles in more than a hundred countries. They have performed before kings and popes. They have played on mountainsides in rural Italy, in a bullring in France that was still slick with blood, and in every city in America with a high school gym. Wherever they appeared, the Harlem Globetrotters always played in front of capacity crowds. During the NBA's lean years the owners would implore Saperstein to schedule the Globetrotters in their buildings as "preliminary" games to NBA contests. Saperstein consequently wielded enough financial clout to keep the NBA white until 1950. By that time Jackie Robinson was already an American institution and the NBA's racial imbalance was much too obvious. Saperstein relented, and the Boston Celtics drafted Chuck Cooper, a 6'5", light-skinned rebounder from Duquesne. In a later round the Washington Capitols picked 6'8" Earl Lloyd from West Virginia State. Saperstein also demonstrated the depth of his brotherly love by selling one of his aging stars—Clifton Nathaniel, aka Nathaniel ("Sweetwater") Clifton—to the New York Knicks for a handsome price. Cooper, Lloyd, and Clifton all proved to be solid ballplayers with a penchant for the spectacular, and the fans clamored for more. Saperstein was eventually persuaded to allow a quota system in the NBA, and three blacks per team was the limit in the mid-1950s. Scores of talented black players like Cal Ramsey from NYU, Cleo Hill from Winston-Salem State, and Stacey Arceneaux from Taft High School were early victims of the NBA's racial proscription. As soon as the league started turning a profit on its own product, Saperstein's influence began to fade. By the early 1960s the quota was up to five blacks per team. It was an unwritten law that an NBA coach could play three blacks at home, four on the road, and five when the team was losing. Then Abe Saperstein died in 1966, and within ten years the NBA was 80 percent black.

The media is still white, most of the cash customers are still white, and all of the owners are still white: but the NBA's entire cultural ambience is now black. Because white players are now in the minority, they sometimes receive more playing time, publicity, and financial remuneration than their talents warrant. This disproportion causes much of the racial animosity in the NBA. Only a fifth of the league is white, yet more than 95 percent of the fistfights are between black and white ballplayers.

Wally Jones was excluded from the 1964 USA Olympic Basketball Team because of a racial quota, but he went on to play in the NBA for ten years. "To me," says Jones, "black basketball means just reacting to the game. White basketball is always more predictable, especially on offense. A guy like Pete Maravich has made a career of copying what blacks have always been doing. Pete's still learning, but he's white, so he's a superstar. I'm not saying that Maravich isn't a good ballplayer. I just think the cat is too studied. He can't make those unknown moves like The Pearl or Dr. J. Underneath all the mechanics, white offense is straight up and down."

The differences between white basketball and black basketball are environmental, not genetic, but they can also be complementary. . . . Bill Bradley has run nearly 150 yards in the last nineteen seconds, but the Knicks' intricate pattern has yet to shake loose an open shot. Bradley reads the 24-second clock with alarm and immediately unloads the ball to Earl Monroe—who fakes, fidgets, and burrows boldly into the middle. Three defenders attack Monroe and kill his dribble, and all his avenues seem to be blocked. Until Monroe leaves his feet with a quantum quiver. . . . And a single bony arm escapes from the trap, to shoot a spinning 10-footer that snaps through the basket and tangles the net on a rainbow. . . .

7

"… FOR UPON ALL THE GLORY SHALL BE A DEFENSE"

In 1956 the Dodgers were still in Brooklyn, and the Lakers were in Minneapolis; Howdy Doody was America's favorite baby-sitter, and everybody loved Lucy. And in the springtime of the year William Felton Russell was a twenty-two-year-old, 6'9", 215-pound basketball visionary and revolutionary. Russell was always much stronger than his lithe body suggested. And he had flawless timing, total dedication, and an overwhelming presence on defense. In Russell's junior and senior years at the University of San Francisco, he led the team to 55 consecutive victories and back-to-back NCAA championships. Even though he could neither shoot nor dribble, Russell was a certified two-time wire-service All-American. But sporting events that originated on the West Coast were rarely seen in the East, and NCAA basketball championships didn't rate national television coverage until 1963. The official statistics revealed that Russell was a mere thirty-first on the '55–'56 NCAA scoring parade and was only the fourth ranking rebounder. A large number of influential basketball experts who had never seen Russell play expressed grave doubts about his true ability. Russell was also black, thoughtful, and strong-willed, so most NBA observers agreed he was a bad risk.

As the 1956 NBA collegiate draft drew nigh, the Harlem Globetrotters made Russell a public offer of $50,000 a year to tour with them (although Abe Saperstein's actual bid was less than half that amount). "Before I even think about turning pro," said Russell, "I'm going to play on the United States Olympic Basketball Team in Melbourne, Australia." The '56–'57 NBA season was scheduled to commence on October 27, and because Australia is in the Southern Hemisphere, where the seasons are reversed, the Olympic competition was scheduled from mid-November to early December. For a variety of reasons, the pros were leery of chancing a valuable number-one draft pick on Bill Russell.

Only three of the eight existing NBA franchises were interested: the Rochester Royals, who had the first choice in the lottery, the Minneapolis Lakers with the third selection, and the Boston Celtics with number six. A real-estate millionaire named Walter Brown owned the Celtics, and Brown was wise enough to rubber-stamp all of coach Red Auerbach's basketball decisions. And Auerbach was in a fever over Russell. "Even as a collegian," says Auerbach, "Bill Russell was the most important basketball player in the country. I *had* to get him for the Celtics."

Rochester ultimately decided it simply could not afford the $25,000 salary that Russell was reportedly demanding, and the Royals were planning to draft Sihugo Green, a muscular one-on-one guard from Duquesne. The St. Louis Hawks had the league's number-two selection, but owner Ben Kerner wanted no part of Russell for several reasons: 6'9" Bob Pettit was the Hawks' resident gate attraction, Kerner also balked at Russell's price tag, and St. Louis was the last all-white team in the NBA.

Minneapolis was poised to pick Russell when Auerbach placed a momentous telephone call to Ben Kerner. "I'm not going to waste your time," said Auerbach. "I'll trade you Ed Macauley for your first draft pick."

Easy Ed Macauley was a 6'8", 190-pound, All-Star center with a deadly one-hander and an unstoppable hook shot. Macauley was also frail, sick, and contemplating retirement at age twenty-eight. But the irresistible attraction of Auerbach's proposal was that Macauley had been twice an All-American at St. Louis University. Kerner knew that the Hawk fans would welcome Macauley back home like a prodigal son. Auerbach was shrewd, but Kerner realized that the Celtics' coach was also on a string. "It's a deal," said Kerner. "If you throw in Cliff Hagan."

Cliff Hagan was a burly 6'4" forward who had teamed with Frank Ramsey to lead the University of Kentucky to an undefeated season back in '53–'54. Immediately after their graduation both Hagan and Ramsey were called into military service for a two-year stretch. In the 1954 collegiate draft Auerbach had gone ahead and drafted Hagan and Ramsey anyway, and his peers called him a fool. "You really want Hagan?" Auerbach muttered into the receiver. Then he smiled and slowly torched a prize cigar. "It breaks my heart, Ben. But you got him."

The '56–'57 Boston Celtics were a formidable ball club even without Russell. The team's strength was provided by Bob Cousy, Bill Sharman, and rookie Tommy Heinsohn, three gunners who shot first and never asked questions. The Celtics were 16–8 when Russell finally joined them on December 22, 1956, for a game against the St. Louis Hawks. Russell played twenty-one minutes and registered 6 points and 16 rebounds. Macauley totaled 17 points and 9 rebounds, and Hagan made only a cursory appearance as the Celtics prevailed, 95–93, on clutch baskets by Sharman and Heinsohn. Nobody suspected a thing, but the revolution was already under way.

Cousy and Sharman were juggernauts on offense and weaklings on defense, so the experts predicted that Russell's defensive orientation would create unsolvable technical and personal problems. But Russell stayed out of everybody's way when the Celtics had the ball, and he played a one-man zone defense that prohibited lay-ups and intimidated short jumpers. The team was joyously transfigured in a fortnight, and four months later they faced the Hawks in the seventh game of the NBA's championship series. Pettit scored 39, Macauley had 9, and Hagan got 24 points. Russell managed only 19 points, but he reaped 32 rebounds, and the Celtics won, 125–123, in double overtime. Nobody knew it, but the revolution was already accomplished.

Such as they were, the NBA's fortunes had been built by the scoring heroics of players like Joe Fulks, George Mikan, and Wilt Chamberlain. And everybody knew that the team with the most points always won the game. In the late 1950s and early 1960s the NBA game was almost totally offensive: On February 27, 1959, the Celtics beat the Minneapolis Lakers by the whopping score of 173–146. Over the course of the '61–'62 season six players averaged over 30 points a game—Wilt Chamberlain (50.4), Elgin Baylor (38.3 over 48 ball games), Walt Bellamy (31.6), Bob Pettit (31.1), Jerry West (30.8), and Oscar Robertson (30.3). Then, on December 2, 1962, Philadelphia outlasted New York, 169–147, in a contest that saw Chamberlain shoot a miraculous 28–32 from the foul line and tally 100 points all by himself. NBA teams regularly averaged 120 points a game, and the scoreboards popped and flashed like pinball machines. The fans were impressed, then dazed, and finally bored.

Bill Sharman retired in 1961, and discounting an ill-advised 7-game stint as player-coach of the Cincinnati Royals in 1969, Bob Cousy bronzed his sneakers in 1963. Auerbach was quick to surround Russell with defensive demons like Tom Sanders and K. C. Jones, and the Celtics became the first team in the NBA to pay its players for doing other things besides scoring points. Only twice in Russell's thirteen-year playing career would the Celtics fail to gain the NBA title. . . .

Don Ohl brings the ball slowly upcourt for the Detroit

Pistons. Ohl's dribble is tentative, and as he approaches midcourt, K. C. Jones jumps at him and swarms on his right hand. Ohl switches his dribble, dumps the ball to teammate Eddie Miles, and tries to run away from Jones. . . . Miles is a better jump shooter than Ohl, but "The Man with the Golden Arm" is an inferior ball handler. "Run a play!" shouts Charlie Wolf, the Pistons' coach. "Run the post series!"

"Post two!" Miles yells to his teammates. "Post two!" A play designed to spring Ohl for a jump shot.

But John Havlicek bellies up to Miles in the backcourt, and the Pistons need eight seconds to bring the ball across the time line. Miles hauls up his dribble with relief and looks to initiate the play with a pass to Ray Scott. . . . The Pistons' center is at his proper station above the foul line, but Bill Russell is on Scott's back like a cat on a screen door. The play is jammed, and the shot clock is down to 13. . . . Miles protects the ball from Havlicek and looks instead for help. . . . Bailey Howell, the Pistons' All-Star forward, shuffles toward Miles but can't quite push his way clear of Tom Sanders's long-limbed resistance. . . . Away from the ball, in the weak-side corner, 6'8", 240-pound Bob Ferry and 6'7", 230-pound Tommy Heinsohn beat each other up in total privacy. . . . Don Ohl floats through the remains of the play and reemerges from the pack to see Havlicek and Jones both harassing the unfortunate Miles. "Here!" Ohl shouts, and Miles gladly flings him the ball. The clock is at 7, and Ohl is 35 feet from the basket. . . . Ohl dribbles once to his right and is chested to a standstill by Sanders. At the same time Havlicek completes the switch by blocking Ohl's passing lane to Howell. . . . But Howell is a cagey veteran: He fakes Havlicek toward the ball; then he pivots and heads for the basket. Ohl picks up the move and leads Howell to the rim with a perfect looping pass. . . . But Russell sniffs out the play and leaps away from Scott. Russell arrives just in time to fingertip the pass off the backboard and into the far corner. . . . Bob Ferry alertly runs down the loose ball and heaves a wild fadeaway hook shot just under the buzzer. . . . The Pistons are in complete disarray, but while the ball is still in flight, Jones, Havlicek, and Sanders bump their men and take off downcourt. . . . The shot misses, and Russell claws the rebound. Then Russell tosses a nifty outlet pass to Jones, and the Celtics are three-on-two against Miles and Ohl. . . . Jones takes the ball to the foul line and kicks it to the cutting Havlicek, who dribbles once and then slides a pass to Sanders for an uncontested lay-up. . . .

"Bill Russell and the Celtics proved one thing," says Al Attles, coach and GM of the Golden State Warriors. "That a great defense can generate a great fast-break offense all by itself. The best offense in the world can have a bad night when the shots aren't falling. Over an entire season it's always easier for a team to maintain defensive consistency. Russell showed that it takes defense to win championships."

Most of the current NBA teams still operate under the old dispensation and allow their offense to determine the shape of their defense. Fast-break teams want to accelerate the tempo of a game and always use aggressive defenses. A press fosters instant decisions and nervous passes. Even if it compels no turnovers, a good press can make an offense struggle just to bring the ball upcourt. The more time a pattern team needs to set up its offense, the more it has to hurry its plays. So there are full-court presses which attack the inbounds pass. There are three-quarter-court presses which permit the inbounds pass and then double-team the recipient. There are half-court presses which lure the ball into the forecourt and then pin it against the midcourt line. There are zone presses and man-to-man presses. "Off the record," says a black assistant coach, "we always use a zone press against black ball handlers and a man-to-man press against white players. The white players have better fundamentals and can usually handle complicated pressure defenses better than the blacks." A press is also used when a team is on the short end of a rout or when the game clock is running down and a win depends upon a successful gamble.

When fast-break teams play each other, there's rarely any need for a press. An all-out running ball game can be a prancing of stallions and a leaping of dolphins, styled with a quick lizard's grace. But nothing can dull a good running ball game faster than a high count of turnovers. The running game gets sloppy and erratic whenever the players are jet-lagged or careless.

Pattern teams like to play a much more passive defense than a running team, usually some kind of zone. In a theoretical zone defense, each defensive player guards an assigned area of the court, picking up whatever offensive player comes through and then letting him go when he leaves. In a man-to-man defense, each defender covers a specific offensive player wherever he goes. "Man-to-man is the toughest defense to play," says Dave Cowens, "and when it's played correctly, it's the toughest to beat. Every player is responsible for guarding a man by himself, so you can appeal to a player's pride and competitive spirit. When an opponent scores or gets an offensive rebound against a zone defense, the defenders can always blame a teammate for the breakdown. There's no direct personal responsibility in a fancy zone defense."

A zone defense clogs the crucial area near the basket and will concede most shots taken from 20–25 feet. In the point-happy 1960s most NBA offenses were satisfied with creating one-on-one or two-on-two situations, and playing defense was relatively simple. "All you had to do," says Rod Thorn, an eight-year NBA vet and currently the GM of the Chicago Bulls, "was to play your man straight up and get over an occasional pick. There was little defensive helping out back then, and a bad defensive player was always exploited. But these days a guy with problems on defense can be hidden inside a zone." A zone defense also affords superior rebounding position while at the same time protecting the rebounders from accumulating fouls. "Another big reason why zones are so effective in the NBA," says Larry Brown, ex-coach of the Denver Nuggets, "is that teams don't practice much against them. If they did, the pros are such great shooters and passers that they would destroy even the best zones. But playing offense against a zone encourages bad habits. Nobody cuts, nobody sets picks, and everybody looks first for the outside shot."

The zone defense, of course, is illegal in the NBA. "It's a zone," says John Nucatola, a Hall of Fame referee, "if a defensive center plays more than eight feet away from his man, and if the same defensive player remains in the three-second lane for more than three seconds." Nucatola also explains that "zones" are punishable by a warning and then a technical foul, but that "position defenses" are allowed. Tommy Heinsohn laughs at the suggestion. "The Atlanta Hawks play a very radical position defense," rasps Heinsohn. "A two-one-two zone. The same kind that's used by every high school team in the country."

But pure zone or pure man-to-man is rarely the issue since most pro teams use combination defenses that employ both principles. Even the most orthodox man-to-man gets into zone activities when two defenders suddenly trade assignments by calling "switch," when they drop back to give a poor shooter room, or when they "help out" against a freewheeling center. The NBA has changed the wording of its no-zone rules several times in an attempt to refine exactly what is permissible, but the fluid nature and high speed of the game make precise rulings impossible. "The referees are very inconsistent about calling zones," says Hubie Brown, coach of the Hawks. "Most refs don't have the guts to make the call. But Richie Powers once slapped us with a zone technical against Portland when Bill Walton hadn't even come across the midcourt line yet. It was a 1-point game at the time, and we wound up losing by 3. The entire situation is absurd."

Richie Powers is the senior official in the NBA with twenty years of service. He believes that the league's antizone law is "antiquated" and should be repealed because of common usage. Before a game played on March 1, 1978, between the New Jersey Nets and the Atlanta Hawks, Powers summoned the captains and the coaches. "Look, fellas," said Powers. "I know that both of your teams play a lot of exotic defenses. Well, tonight I'm not going to penalize either of you if you do play them." Powers was the ball game's "lead official" and under NBA procedure the only one who could take action against any defense played in violation of Rule 12, Section I. Both teams used undisguised zones frequently throughout the game, the shooting percentages were below normal—.407 for the Hawks and .404 for the Nets—and New Jersey won, 97–95. NBA commissioner Larry O'Brien responded to the news by fining Powers $2,500 and suspending him without pay for three games. "The job of a referee," said O'Brien, "is to enforce the existing playing rules to the best of his ability, not to arbitrarily set aside those rules to suit his own views."

The NBA's Board of Governors still equates zone defenses with long train rides, dull ball games, and empty stands. But the proliferation of "illegal" zones has drastically changed the game. High-scoring pivot men like Kareem Abdul-Jabbar have been rendered obsolete by constant double- and triple-teaming. "One of these years," says Bill Melchionni, a seven-year player in the NBA and ABA and onetime GM of the Nets, "the NBA is going to have to make a decision about the zone. I'd personally like to see them put in the three-point shot that we had in the ABA. That would force the defense to play the guards tough. And it would prevent sagging and clogging the middle. The ABA also had a thirty-second shot clock that gave an offense more time to work the ball and stretch out a zone defense. But the prospects are bleak." The 3-point show reminds the NBA too much of its own carnival days, and the Board would never tamper with the primeval sanctity of the 24-second clock. So instead of dealing with the problem, Larry O'Brien makes righteous pronouncements about the law, and the NBA's game officials are forced to be hypocrites.

The most common NBA zone is a two-three formation in which the two guards play a switching man-to-man and the three big men play a straight zone. Every ball club in the league uses some form of zone against a one-on-one offense. "Did you ever try and dribble against a good zone?" asks Tommy Heinsohn. "It's a bitch." Most zones try to nudge the offense to one side of the court and then trap the ball in the corner. From 1968 to 1976 Dick Motta's Chicago Bulls were especially adept at cutting the court in half on an offense; Norm Van Lier fed his family by hiding in the weeds near the top of the key and gobbling up any attempts to reverse the ball.

A team with a dynamic big man at its hub can afford to play a two-two-one or funnel zone. This variation denies the pass to the corners and keeps the middle wide open, forcing the offense into the jaws of a Bill Russell, Wilt Chamberlain, or Nate Thurmond. A funnel zone can usually eat any offense alive, depending upon the size, quality, and defensive appetite of the big man.

Any ball game matching a break-press team against a pattern-zone team is usually played in spurts as each team temporarily succeeds in establishing its own pace. A disciplined pattern-zone team might have a slight advantage because deliberate offenses yield only high percentage shots and tend to minimize the number of defensive rebounds. Good offensive rebounding can also cramp a running team by making both backboards competitive and consequently delaying the outlet pass. Once a defensive rebound has already been relinquished, some teams have a big man hang around for several beats to crowd the rebounder and, they hope, stall his pass. Most breaking teams look for the same triggerman on every break, and another defensive strategy has a player linger on the outskirts of the outlet lane as he retreats on defense—looking for an interception, but settling for a hesitation.

In order for a running team to be controlled, teamwide defensive hustle is absolutely mandatory. It takes about four seconds to cover the 90 feet from one end of the court to the other, so if a defense can hold off a two-on-one or three-on-two for only two seconds, the rest of the team has a chance to catch up with the play. "The break is over once the big men get back on defense," says Tommy Heinsohn. "The big men can block shots and crumple bodies. So now the best thing you've got left is a jump shot."

Zone defenses can be stymied by good long-range shooting, but seldom on a consistent enough basis to win a championship. The New York Knicks of '69–'70 and '72–'73 were exceptions only because Willis Reed, Earl Monroe, Walt Frazier, Dave DeBusschere, Bill Bradley, Cazzie Russell, and Jerry Lucas were all magnificent shooters. Overloading is another technique used to confound a zone defense. One area is simply flooded with two men, forcing the defender to make a choice; then the ball is moved to the open man. "Quick, sharp passes can beat a zone," informs Tommy Heinsohn. "There's no man alive who ever outran a good pass. But the very best way to whip a zone is to get the ball the hell upcourt before the zone has a chance to organize."

A ball game is always downright brutal whenever two pattern teams collide. Since neither team is running, lay-ups can usually be earned only off the offensive boards, and play is apt to be intense, turbulent, and low-scoring. "The team that wants it more will win," says Phil Jackson. "The team that believes more in its own purpose."

Pattern-zone teams will hardly ever blow out an opponent the way fast-break teams can, but Red Auerbach cautions against placing undue emphasis on final scores. "You win by 1 point," says Auerbach, "or you win by 20. What's the difference? Maybe you suffer more in a close ball game, but they all count the same. What is important is when you win and how often. And you can't win consistently without a good defense. It all comes back to that. When I was coaching the Celtics, we spent eighty percent of every practice on defense. I know that a lot of people think that the defense in the NBA stinks. But let me tell you something: If it was really bad, then the teams in the league would average 160 points a game."

Transition basketball is the parenthesis between defense and offense and defense. "When the Celtics scout the colleges," says Tommy Heinsohn, "That's where they look to find a player's heart." The easiest transition is from defense to offense: A bad pass, a steal, a loose ball, or a defensive rebound, and presto chango . . . suddenly the good guys have a chance to score. An experienced player can often anticipate a change of fortune and cheat a few steps downcourt. This can give a fast-break team a devastating edge.

The most challenging transition is from offense to defense. The guards are tempted to loiter on the offensive perimeter, looking to pick off a careless pass. The big men jerk to a halt, then make a sighing, rolling pivot before loping downcourt to play defense. "There's no skill involved in getting back on defense," says Portland's Bobby Gross. "You just need a willingness to do it." Gross surprised many NBA watchers with his brilliant performance opposite Julius Erving in the 1977 championship series. Gross shot an indisputable 67 percent from the field and did a highly respectable job of containing The Doctor. "Erving is an incredible ballplayer," says Gross, "but he's in a position where he has to bear the burden of most of the 76ers' offense. We just made him pay at the other end. Especially during the offense-to-defense transition. That's why most of my shots were either fast-break lay-ups or wide-open fifteen-footers. There are a lot of guys like Erving who get caught under the basket and make no effort to get downcourt at all. Most of these guys are only interested in scoring points, and they're forever looking to save themselves for offense."

Bill Russell is now a very rich and famous man, and his revolutions and revelations are long forgotten. Russell owns rubber plantations in Africa. Sometimes he does "color" commentary for a prime-time college basketball game. Once in a while he even guest-hosts "The Tonight Show." And these days Russell plays his hoops for Bell Telephone. He's strictly a shooter now, and he plays in civvies and shoes while seated on a desk: Russell casually hits another over-the-head bank shot from 40 feet. Then he laughs, claps his hands, and cackles commercial messages into the camera's blind red eye.

8
THE LITTLE MEN

In 1968 Ben Kerner sold the St. Louis Hawks to a group of Atlanta businessmen for $3.5 million. The price included 6'5", 195-pound Joe Caldwell—a mediocre shooter, who was fast enough to eat Walt Frazier's lunch anytime he was hungry. The Hawks' other starting guard was 6'2", 190-pound Walt Hazzard—a penetrator, passer, and scorer, who was quick rather than fast. At one forward was 6'5", 210-pound Lou Hudson—a remarkable shooter who averaged over 25 ppg four times in his career. Bill Bridges was the muscle forward at 6'6" and 235 pounds—a lightweight shooter, who big-shouldered his way to over 1,000 rebounds a year in his prime. At center was Zelmo Beaty, a good-shooting 6'9", 230-pounder who could barely jump 2 inches off the floor. "I think Zelmo had about five knee operations," recalls Steve Patterson, a five-year pro out of UCLA. "But there was nothing wrong with Zelmo's elbows. He was strong, experienced, and downright mean. I know plenty of guys who used to toss and turn the night before they had to bang heads with Z." Jim Davis at 6'10", 230 pounds, and Paul Silas at 6'6", 235 pounds, were the first big men off the bench. Don Ohl was the backup guard, while 6'4", 210-pound Richie

Guerin functioned as the team's fourth guard, coach, and unofficial general manager.

"It was quite a challenge to be in a spot like that," says Guerin. "And I enjoyed the daylights out of it. When you're a player, your first responsibility is to motivate yourself. As a player-coach, my first priority was to try to motivate the whole team. I didn't have time to think about myself. And because I was still playing, it was easy for me to relate to the guys on the team. I had to be willing and able to go out and do everything I asked them to do. Late practices. Extra laps. But I could coach the team by example and I could provide on-court leadership. It was much more relaxing than just being a bench coach because I could work out all my frustrations by playing." These days Guerin is a successful stockbroker and color man for the Knicks' radio broadcasts. "There was no such thing as an assistant coach back then," he says. "If I was in the game, one of the veterans would make the substitutions. We all got along, and we had a very good ball club."

In the Hawks' first season in Atlanta, the team was 48–34 and placed second in the Western Division, 7 games behind the Chamberlain-Baylor-West LA Lakers. In the play-offs the Hawks lasted until the semifinals before being blown out 4–1 by the mighty Lakers. But insiders weren't fooled. The Hawks were an exciting, fluent blend of talent, and Guerin was a combative leader. Los Angeles was getting old in a hurry, and the next dynasty seemed to be germinating in Georgia. There was a ground swell of local support for the Hawks; but the Omni wouldn't be ready for another four years, and all home games were played in the Georgia Tech field house, which seated only 6,500. The Hawks averaged 6,200 fans in '68–'69, and every one of them knew straight off that Caldwell, Hazzard, Hudson, Bridges, Beaty, Davis, and Silas were black.

During the off season the Hawks' corporate ownership peddled the brawny Silas for a white journeyman forward named Gary Gregor. "There was nothing I could do about that one," sighs Guerin. The team was shaken again when Beaty announced his intention of sitting on his option clause for the '69–'70 season and then signing with the Utah Stars of the ABA. Guerin started dialing the telephone, and he didn't hang up until he traded the ubiquitous "Player to Be Named Later" to the Detroit Pistons for the wistful Walter Bellamy. "Bells" was an awesome physical specimen at 6'11" and 265 pounds; when he was ringing, he could outplay anyone from Bill Russell to Wilt Chamberlain and back. But Bellamy was shy by nature and much more likely to seek invisibility.

"I never had any problems with Bellamy," says Guerin. "He was comfortable in Atlanta, and we got along just fine. Bellamy played some of the best ball of his career with the Hawks. He did everything I asked. That second year in Atlanta was my last one as an active player. We had such a good season that I limited myself to playing in only eight ball games." With Bellamy plugging the middle, the Hawks compiled another 48–34 record in '69–'70. This time it was good enough for a divisional championship by a margin of 2 games over the Lakers. But then the Hawks were swept by LA in the second round of postseason play. The Omni was still three years from completion, home attendance hovered at 6,100, and Atlanta's mandarins decided that the survival of the franchise depended on a White Hope.

Fortunately the 1970 collegiate draft offered a pair of likely prospects: Rudy Tomjanovich, a 6'8" scoring forward, who had diligently shattered most of Cazzie Russell's scoring records at Michigan. And Pistol Pete Maravich, a 6'5", 200-pound backcourt ace from Louisiana State University, who had led the country in scoring from 1967 to 1970 with averages of 43.8, 44.2, and 44.5. Maravich's floppy socks, bouncing locks, innovative passes, and fanciful shots had already made him basketball's biggest gate attraction.

Unfortunately the '69–'70 Hawks had the fourth best record in the NBA, so their chances of landing either Tomjanovich or

Maravich were slim. But Guerin rode the phones again, and a few hours before the trading deadline he came up with a doozy: The San Francisco Warriors were a decimated ball club which had managed only 30 victories. Their star forward, Rick Barry, had run off to the ABA, and their All-Star center, Nate Thurmond, had played only half the season because of knee trouble. The Warriors' owner, Franklin Mieuli, was desperate for a big man and a drawing card. For some unknown reason, Mieuli believed he could sign Zelmo Beaty to a contract before Beaty became a free agent and signed with Utah. Mieuli presented the astonished Guerin with the Warriors' top draft pick, as well as a hard-nosed, rebounding forward named Clyde Lee, in exchange for the NBA rights to Beaty. "Zelmo did sign with Utah," says Guerin, "so we got something for nothing. We were planning to use our new draft choice on Tomjanovich." But the Detroit Pistons picked first and tabbed Bob Lanier, the San Diego Rockets selected Tomjanovich, and the Hawks went for Maravich. Amid much ballyhoo, Atlanta signed Maravich to a multiyear contract worth a reported $1.9 million.

As a rookie Maravich averaged 23.2 points per game and inspired raves, gasps, and SRO crowds all over the league. But the Hawks finished 10 games below .500, and home attendance dwindled to 5,979 fans a game. "A lot of guys on the team resented Maravich," Guerin says. "Joe Caldwell asked for a million-dollar contract, and when he was turned down, he jumped to the ABA. A lot of guys resented the nutty things that Maravich did on the court . . . like triggering a three-on-one break and throwing a silly behind-the-back pass into the seats. Pete was also bad on defense. Real bad. He was a nice kid, but most of the older players resented his money. Both Maravich and Hazzard needed the ball to be effective, and Hazzard was insecure and almost useless for the entire season because he knew he would be the next to go." The disastrous '70–'71 season concluded with the Hawks getting trounced 4–1 by New York in the opening round of the play-offs. During the off-season Hazzard, Bridges, and Davis were disposed of in a series of transactions that brought Don May, Herm Gilliam, Larry Siegfried, and Don Adams to Atlanta. The budding dynasty was ravaged, and the promise of a championship was a lie. Over the next two seasons the Hawks won 82 and lost 82 and were easily pushed aside early in the play-offs. The Pistol continued to smoke—19.3 and 26.1 ppg—but the team drew an average crowd of only 7,700 during its first season in the Omni.

Guerin officially became Atlanta's general manager in 1972, and his first act was to hire Cotton Fitzsimmons to coach the team. But the Hawks kept falling through the league, and both Guerin and Maravich were soon sent packing. "A guy named Bill Putnam owned ten percent of the Hawks," explains Guerin. "He also served as the president and chief operator of both the Hawks and the Atlanta Flames, a hockey team. Putnam was a solid professional with a knowledgeable background in sports. We became good friends. Then, in 1973, the other owners decided to remove Putnam as chief operator and replace him with a southern gentleman who knew nothing about basketball. I told the owners they were making a big mistake. They felt I was a threat to their authority, and three weeks later I was canned even though I had four years remaining on my contract. The guy who replaced Putnam was the same guy who drafted Marvin Webster and David Thompson in 1975 and couldn't sign or trade either of them. But I'm delighted to be out of the business. There's more politics than basketball in the NBA."

A year after Guerin's dismissal, Maravich and his hefty contract were dealt to the expansion New Orleans Jazz for Dean Meminger, a crippled Bob Kauffman, and a batch of future draft choices. In '74–'75 Maravich averaged 21.5 and asked his fans if they were "still using that greasy kid stuff." Two years later The Pistol won the NBA's scoring title with 31.1 a game, and the sportswriters picked Maravich and Paul Westphal as the NBA's finest guards. And millions of basketball buffs believe that Pete Maravich is the greatest guard who ever played the game. . . .

The Jazz are in Madison Square Garden against the Knicks,

and Maravich is pitted against Jim Cleamons. As Maravich dribbles toward midcourt, the ball seems to glow and flash like a golden coin. The Pistol shows the ball in his right hand, then whips it behind his back and between his legs before it suddenly reappears in his left hand. The fans are mesmerized, and Maravich crosses the midcourt line. When he reaches the top of the key, Maravich begins faking in earnest, but Cleamons steadfastly overplays his opponent's right hand. The ball wiggles and pulsates under The Pistol's command—he fakes left, fakes left again, and wants to go right. But Cleamons will not be duped—his left arm sweeps the floor to Maravich's right, and his right arm guards the passing lane.

The Jazz's center, Rich Kelley, sets a 7-foot, 250-pound pick just above the foul line, "Pick left, Clem!" shouts Lonnie Shelton, the Knicks' center. Cleamons glances at Kelley, then scrambles and beats Maravich to the crossroads. Cut off, Maravich retreats and dribbles back to his left. With only three seconds on the shot clock, The Pistol launches a hasty 25-footer that snaps off the back rim and into Shelton's hands. Cleamons races downcourt, but Maravich doesn't make it back on defense until Shelton's fast-break dunk shot has already bounced three times.

In the first half Cleamons steals two of Maravich's passes, blocks two of his shots, and holds him to two field goals in twelve tries. New Orleans has no other game plan, and the Knicks lead by 10 at intermission. The second half brings more of the same: Maravich monopolizes the ball; but he can't go right, and he can't buy a basket. He tries to compensate by looking to pass instead of shoot; but his teammates are used to standing around, and the Jazz's offense remains lumpish. In the meantime, Cleamons is all over the court: bustling, ball handling, defending, rebounding, and subtly greasing the Knicks' offense. New York still leads by 10 going into the stretch when Maravich finally connects on two consecutive shots. Willis Reed immediately replaces two rookies with Bob McAdoo and Lonnie Shelton, and the Knicks run off 6 straight points to ice the game. New Orleans flurries near the buzzer, but New York wins, 108–105. Maravich has recorded 40 minutes, 9 assists, and 11 points on the back of 4–20 from the field. . . .

There's no doubt that Maravich is a better shooter than Cleamons. But Maravich has been thrust into a situation where he must force a lot of shots and score a lot of points or else his team will lose. On the other hand, Cleamons can afford to attempt only those shots he knows he can make and consequently has the higher lifetime shooting percentage. "Nobody can win in the NBA with a guard controlling the ball as much as Maravich does," says Jack Ramsay. "Without him New Orleans is dreadful. With him, the best they can do is break even." Discounting the '74–'75 expansion season, Maravich played in a total of 185 ball games from 1975 to 1978; New Orleans was 19–42 with The Pistol out of the lineup and 93–92 when he played. The team is programmed to showcase Pete Maravich, not to win, and New Orleans is always among the league leaders in home attendance.

The Pistol digs what he does, but he does what he's told. "I'd do anything to win a championship," Maravich says. "I'd change my whole game. If I could ever play with someone like Jabbar, I'd be happy to be his caddy." Jim Cleamons is a jack-of-all-trades and master of most. Pete Maravich is a media Frankenstein, a sensitive soul trapped in an absurd role that brings as much frustration as glory. Every team in the NBA needs considerable offensive punch from its backcourt, but a ball club is always better off if the starting guards average 20 and 15 points than if they score 32 and 8. Professional basketball is ultimately a big man's game, and when a guard is a team's primary scorer, the ball dallies in the backcourt, and the big men feel like orphans. Even the marvelous Oscar Robertson— the greatest all-around guard who ever laced a sneaker—didn't win a championship until he sublimated his scoring and teamed with Kareem Abdul-Jabbar in Milwaukee in 1971.

"Pete Maravich is a great scorer," says Bob Kauffman, now

the GM of the Detroit Pistons. "He's the best with the ball, and he's certainly the flashiest guard in the league. Because he plays with so much flair, he sometimes looks better than he really is. It's important for a guard to be a well-balanced player because the guard position is the most complex in the game."

All basketball players have special responsibilities in the offensive, defensive, and transitional phases of the game. But every team needs a player who can safely conduct the ball across the midcourt line. "Ball-handling guards" are usually small, fast, and quick. At 5'11" and 175 pounds, Mack Calvin is a ball-handling guard who specializes in the running game. Calvin's moderately priced services are always in demand, and he has lasted for nine years in the NBA and ABA with eight different teams. . . . Calvin dribbles comfortably in full stride, his right hand low as he juggles the ball hard against the floor. The ball game is just under way, and the Denver Nuggets' fast break is rolling. Calvin flicks his head and sees Bobby Jones flying on one wing and David Thompson on the other. Bob Wilkerson is making up ground and coming hard on Calvin's right hand. Dan Issel, Denver's big man, trails the pack but will shortly be arriving on Calvin's left. . . . Two defenders are back, one is coming, and two are loafing. There is an abundance of shot possibilities. But Calvin chooses to pull up at the foul line and wait for Issel to plow through the lane. Then Calvin rewards the big man with a slick pass and a chance to dunk the ball. Issel creams the shot through the rim, and the ball nearly flattens as it hits the floor. The brawny center hustles back on defense and cocks an appreciative finger in Calvin's direction. . . .

"My role involves a lot of decision making," says Mack Calvin. "I'm a field general like a quarterback, only football is static while I have to read and react on the run. The most fundamental duty of a ball-handling guard is to make sure that the big men get going early in the ball game. The old cliché is that if you can get your big men involved at the start, they're going to play better basketball. And it's true. Forwards and centers usually play closer to the basket than guards, so they have to be fed the ball. The big men have a tendency to be lazy if they don't get the ball and score right away. If I can set them up in the beginning of a ball game, the next thing I know they're blocking shots and rebounding like crazy. This starts the fast break going and gets the small men running and into the middle of the action. In basketball, you always get back whatever you give up."

Most big men have little idea which of the opponents' guards are on the court, but a ball-handling guard must be involved with the total ball game. Whenever the fast break is unavailable or inadvisable, a ball-handling guard usually positions the ball and initiates the offense. He has to understand exactly what the coach is thinking, and he has to know all the team's plays. A ball-handling guard must also be aware of the score, the time, who has the hot hand, who has foul trouble, who turns his head on defense, who likes to do what and where he likes to do it.

Clarence "Foots" Walker of the Cleveland Cavaliers is 6'2", 172 pounds, and the epitome of a "penetrating guard." . . . Walker yo-yos the ball at the edge of the Indiana Pacers' two-three zone. The sturdy Walker shifts an eye, dances a hip, and catches a defender leaning the wrong way. In a flash, Walker darts to the basket and flings himself into the bosom of the defense. The Pacers' big men scramble and adjust, and before Walker lands, he is menaced by 6'9" Dan Roundfield and 6'8" Mike Bantom. Still hanging in midair, Walker simulates a shot; then he whips the ball across his body, under Bantom's armpit, and into the waiting hands of teammate Dick Snyder, who pumps it home.

At 6'5" and 210 pounds, Snyder is the classic shooting guard. He can handle well enough to cool out a press, and he plays one-on-one well enough to exploit a smaller defender; but Snyder makes his living playing one-on-none from 20 feet. Like most shooting guards, Snyder is forever anticipating and searching out weak spots in a defense. The more he maneuvers without the ball, the more time he has to set himself and shoot once it comes his way. Long-range shooting has become crucial since the proliferation of zone defenses in the NBA, but good shooting guards are a million dollars a dozen. Unselfish catalysts like Mack Calvin, Foots Walker, Johnny Davis, Dave Twardzik, Norm Van Lier, John Lucas, and Tom Henderson are cheaper and, in the long run, more valuable. "You've got to sacrifice to win in the NBA," says Calvin. "What you usually sacrifice is the ball."

Sometimes a guard is also asked to sacrifice his body. The simplest and most common offensive play in the pro ranks is the guard-forward interchange which requires the little men to set picks on the big men. . . . Don Buse brings the ball upcourt for the Phoenix Suns and calls out a play. Alvan Adams, the Suns' 6'9" center, quickly moves to the top of the key, while forwards Garfield Heard and Walter Davis station themselves in opposite corners. Buse passes the ball to his backcourt partner, Paul Westphal, who relays it over to Adams. . . . The first pass releases Buse, and he runs straight at the man guarding Heard—6'8", 250-pound George McGinnis. Buse stops and braces less than a foot off the bow of Big George's left shoulder. McGinnis pivots and accidentally smashes Buse to the floor, but no whistle blows. . . . Adams passes to Heard, who has danced around the collision and drifted to his favorite spot along the base line. . . . Heard gets an easy shot and a basket, Adams gets an assist, and Buse gets bruised. . . .

If most guards set less intense picks than the doughty Buse, they all know what to do when a big man sets a pick. . . . Wes Unseld is a 6'7", 270-pound post driven deep into the left side of the foul line. Teammate Larry Wright has the ball and the defensive attention of 5'8" Charlie Criss. Wright jukes and dribbles and runs his man into the post. Criss is crossed by Unseld's enormous bulk, and Wright is momentarily unguarded, until Unseld's defender alertly springs out at Wright to deny him the easy jumper. . . . But Wright knows without looking that the contact has sparked the post to life and that Unseld is wheeling to the basket with no one to check him but the diminutive Criss. Wright flips a lob pass, Unseld hits a lay-up, and the pick-and-roll strikes again.

Another species of backcourtsman is the power guard—a physical type, who can shoot from the outlands and drive to the basket on almost anybody. Richie Guerin and Oscar Robertson were the progenitors, while John Williamson and Austin Carr are two of the best modern practitioners. . . . Williamson is 6'2", 215 pounds, bullnecked, and supremely confident. The New Jersey Nets clear out a side, and Super John begins his offensive foray 20 feet from the basket. Williamson relentlessly backs his man closer to the hoop, bumping and thumping, until he suddenly swirls, scowls, and shakes out a jump shot that banks clean from 15. . . . Power guards are always eager to assault the offensive boards and can be used almost like a third forward. Power guards need a great deal of space and ball time to be effective, but they can also provide an offensive boost when they are used sparingly.

In the '77–'78 season Billy Cunningham was the rookie coach of the Philadelphia 76ers, and he took the principle of the power guard to an interesting extreme. The Sixers had a potent brigade of forwards in Julius Erving, George McGinnis, and supersub Steve Mix. There was rarely any leftover playing time for the team's fourth forward, 6'10", 185-pound Joe Bryant. Cunningham solved the problem by judiciously employing Bryant in the backcourt and instructing the other guard to do all the ball handling. Bryant would then position himself some 15–20 feet from the basket, where he was fed with a simple lob pass. Bryant invariably had 5–7 inches on his defender, and he could find a good shot just by turning around and sighting the basket. Bryant was quick enough to avoid getting scorched on defense, but he sat down if he missed four shots in a row.

During the same season the Sixers had another unorthodox power guard in Lloyd Free, the self-styled "All World." Free is only 6'2", but he jumps like a 7-footer, and he loves to run amok in the big man's territory. Free must be reckoned with on the offensive boards, and his 30-foot "moon" shots are either spectacularly accurate or embarrassingly inconsistent.

Defense and consistency are always the better parlay, and the NBA boasts a clutch of premier defensive guards—Jim Cleamons, Dennis Johnson, Butch Beard, Don Chaney, Ted McClain, Gus Bailey, Jim Price, Ed Ratleff, Brian Taylor, Don Buse, Norm Van Lier, and Quinn Buckner. But the active guard with the most All-Defensive Team citations (seven) is Walt Frazier of the Cleveland Cavaliers by way of New York. . . . In his heyday with the Knicks, Frazier was the embodiment of detachment, power, and glamour. He thrived in a crisis and led New York to championships in 1970 and 1973. Frazier was always more accomplished at playing team defense rather than individual defense, so speedsters like Lenny Wilkens, Joe Caldwell, and Randy Smith often singed his eyebrows. But Frazier was strong, intelligent, abundantly gifted, and fortunate to have Willis Reed and Dave DeBusschere behind him to step on his mistakes. The Knick fans were thrilled by Frazier, and they learned to chant "DEE-FENSE!" But Clyde was an unapproachable fantasy as he toured the city's night spots in a purple Rolls-Royce. When the Knicks' "dynasty" began to crumble in '73–'74, Frazier tried to assume more and more offensive responsibility, but the team's fortunes continued to plunge. The Knicks finished out of the play-offs for the next three seasons, and the fans turned and rended Frazier with boos and insults. He became the scapegoat for the team's sad plight, and the turncoat fans applauded in 1977, when Frazier was shipped to Cleveland for Jim Cleamons.

The Cleveland Cavaliers have traditionally been a deliberate ball club that relies on pattern offenses and zone defense, a pace ideally suited to a veteran's legs, and Frazier played well for his new ball club. He took charge of every clutch situation and twice beat the Knicks on last-second baskets. Frazier helped focus his teammates' attention on playing defense, and Cleveland spent large portions of November, December, and January in first place in the Central Division. But Frazier instinctively recoiled from the authoritative mode of coach Bill Fitch, and there was trouble in paradise. "Fitch wants to be the only superstar on the team," Frazier complained. "He doesn't like to be questioned or challenged by any of his players." The rift was rumbling louder and louder until Frazier went down with a foot injury on January 31 in a game against the Lakers. Frazier was never removed from the Cav's active roster, and the foot remained swollen despite conscientious medical attention. When Frazier's disability lingered through the play-offs, Fitch chided him in public for not healing fast enough.

If Frazier's future with Cleveland is in doubt, his accomplishments with the Knicks are indelible. At the "advanced" age of thirty-three, he is steadier, if less spectacular than in his prime, and he still rates among the league's topnotch guards. Frazier has gone through more than a change in geography since he was the toast of Broadway, and he no longer answers to "Clyde." These days Frazier eats natural foods and spends contemplative evenings by the hearth. "I learned my first lesson in survival," says Frazier, "when I realized that nobody in the NBA is physically or mentally strong enough to go all-out on both offense and defense. It's either one or the other, and you have to learn to pick your spots. Another thing I learned very early in my career is that everybody needs help on defense. Even when you're concentrating one hundred percent. Most of the guards in the league have too much talent to be consistently stopped one-on-one. Keeping the ball away from a player is much easier than defending him when he already has it. So if the ball is off to the right and my man goes left, I'll stay on the inside, playing what we call the passing lane. If the guy can't get the ball, there's no way he's going to score no matter how talented he is. When your man does have possession, you try and deny him his favorite direction and you try and make contact with him. If you can push his hip or bump him around, you can limit his freedom of movement. Maybe you can control him. Maybe you can make his shot too soon, or maybe you can force him to adjust while he's shooting. But you always need help."

Position, anticipation, concentration, and control are vital factors in business, marriage, war, and NBA defense. And whatever the enterprise, an indiscreet turning of the head universally invites disaster. . . . The Knicks are hosting the Sixers, and veteran guard Doug Collins is paired against Ray Williams, New York's prize rookie. Collins dribbles lightly toward the left corner, and Williams bounces in tandem, tensing and waiting for Collins to burst to the basket. But Collins lulls the rookie by tossing a leisurely pass to Julius Erving at the top of the key. Collins then ambles toward Erving and draws Williams along for the ride. . . . After only two steps, Williams turns his head to track the ball and breaks eye contact with Collins. The Sixers' All-Star guard bounces off his instincts and reverses field. He cuts behind the rookie, sprints to the hoop, and turns Erving's bounce pass into a lay-up. . . .

Head turning is the most common defensive sin in basketball, and even the most wizened NBA veteran is susceptible. But getting faked off the ground is definitely a tenderfoot mistake. . . . Ray Williams gets busted on a pick and now finds himself guarding Dr. J in the pivot. Julius widens his eyes with delight and nods twice at the basket. The rookie strains, but the first fake sends him high into the air, his long right arm swatting at a phantom basketball. The Doctor's jump shot is halfway through the net by the time Williams lands. . . .

"The only time you ever leave your feet on defense," says Phil Jackson, a pro since 1967, "is when you're positive you can block your man's shot. It takes the average rookie about three years to learn the other players and to feel comfortable in the ball game. There's always something working on one side of the court to make something else happen ten seconds later on the other side of the court, so it's easy to get confused. A rookie's instincts are still conditioned by the college game, and rookies do a lot of guessing. It's always easier to adjust on offense because you know what's supposed to happen, but you pay the full price of inexperience on the other end of the court. Eventually you learn to recognize situations and react without thinking, and then you're right there."

If he's a small man, a rookie must also learn how to cope with the different types of NBA guards: Ball-handling guards are ground into picks and forced to labor on defense. A ball-handling guard can also be taken inside (usually by a power guard), making it difficult for him to get out on the fast break. Shooting guards require man-to-man pressure and are picked up early and overplayed to keep them off the ball. Power guards are severly hampered by zones, and a sliding one-two-two zone can often contain a penetrating guard. "If a penetrating guard is left free to roam the middle," says Gail Goodrich of the New Orleans Jazz, "then he has a lot of options. He can pass left or right, and he can also drive either way. If you let him work his way into a corner and then pin him to the base line, there's only one way he can pass and drive."

Monte Towe is 5'6", Tom Gola is 6'8", and Joe Bryant stands 6'10", but the NBA's "small men" are closest in size to the American norm. "There are more of us to choose from," says Charlie Scott. "So we have to be better athletes than the big men to make it." With such a high level of ability, versatility becomes a deciding factor. Players who can assume a variety of roles get more playing time and are in the middle of more "plays per game" than specialists. But the one essential role of an NBA guard is to use his skills to make his teammates better ballplayers.

The following survey is fashioned after NBA scouting forms and is suggestive rather than definitive:

GUARDS

	BALL HANDLING	PASSING	SPEED	CREATING OWN SHOT	SPOT SHOOTING	SHOT SELECTION	SCORING	EFFECTIVENESS W/O BALL	DEFENSIVE POSITION	DEFENSIVE ANTICIPATION	REBOUNDING	CONSISTENCY	VERSATILITY	DURABILITY	TOTAL
Jerry West	3	3	4	4	4	4	4	4	4	3	4	4	4	4	53
Oscar Robertson	4	4	3	4	4	4	4	2	3	3	4	4	4	4	51
Ralph Beard	4	4	4	3	3	4	3	4	4	4	3	4	3	4	51
Jo Jo White	4	4	3	2	3	4	3	4	4	4	3	4	4	4	50
Bob Wanzer	3	3	3	3	4	4	3	4	4	4	3	4	2	4	48
Richie Guerin	3	4	3	3	4	4	4	3	3	3	3	4	3	4	48
Hal Greer	3	3	4	4	4	4	4	3	3	3	3	4	2	4	48
Gene Shue	4	3	4	4	3	4	4	3	3	3	3	4	2	4	48
Doug Collins	3	3	4	2	4	4	4	4	4	3	3	4	3	2	47
Bill Sharman	3	2	3	2	4	4	4	4	4	3	2	4	3	4	46
Sam Jones	3	2	3	4	4	4	4	3	3	3	3	4	2	4	46
Randy Smith	3	3	4	4	4	3	4	3	2	3	4	3	2	4	46
Bob Cousy	4	4	3	4	3	3	4	1	2	3	3	4	3	4	45
Fred Scolari	3	3	3	3	4	4	4	4	3	3	2	3	2	4	45
Slater Martin	4	4	4	2	3	4	2	4	3	3	2	4	2	4	45
Jim Cleamons	3	3	3	2	3	4	2	3	4	4	4	4	2	4	45
Walt Frazier	3	3	2	4	4	3	4	2	3	3	4	3	3	3	44
George Gervin	3	3	4	4	4	3	4	2	1	1	4	3	4	4	44
Norm Van Lier	4	4	4	3	2	4	2	3	3	4	2	4	2	3	44
Brian Taylor	4	4	4	3	2	3	3	3	3	4	2	3	2	3	43
Lionel Hollins	3	3	4	4	3	2	3	3	3	3	3	3	2	4	43
Pete Maravich	4	4	3	4	4	3	4	1	2	2	3	3	2	4	43
Calvin Murphy	4	3	4	4	4	3	4	2	3	3	1	3	1	4	43
Paul Westphal	3	3	2	4	4	4	4	3	3	3	2	3	2	3	43
David Thompson	2	2	4	4	3	3	4	3	2	3	4	3	3	3	43
Bob Davies	4	3	4	4	3	3	4	2	2	2	2	3	2	4	42
Earl Monroe	4	4	2	4	3	4	4	3	2	2	3	2	2	2	42
Phil Smith	4	3	3	4	4	3	3	2	2	3	3	3	2	3	41
Max Zaslofsky	3	3	2	2	4	4	4	3	2	2	2	3	2	4	40
Carl Braun	2	2	2	4	4	3	4	3	2	2	3	3	2	4	40
Charlie Scott	4	4	4	4	3	3	3	2	2	2	2	2	2	2	39
Dick McGuire	4	4	4	2	1	4	2	2	2	3	2	3	2	4	37
Nate Archibald	4	4	4	4	2	3	4	1	2	2	1	3	1	2	37
Freddie Brown	3	2	3	4	4	2	4	1	2	3	2	2	2	3	36

LEGEND
4 = outstanding   3 = good   2 = average   1 = poor

9
THE BIG LITTLE MEN

There's a fountain spuming in the courtyard of the Plaza Hotel. Across the street, a fleet of horses hitched to hansom cabs shiver and jingle in a late-April breeze. Springtime is glowing with a chemical frenzy, and the hotel's long baroque windows are sealed with monstrous antique curtains. In New York City the Plaza means "class," and rooms overlooking Central Park start at $75 a day. It's always a mild surprise to note that the NBA regularly musters its annual collegiate draft at the Plaza.

The NBA's rented ballroom has the proper number of balustrades and chandeliers, and the unbroken wall opposite the windows is dominated by a huge hand-lettered chart. It is 1962 and the NBA's drafting order lists only nine teams. There are a dais and a microphone in front of the chart, then a spread of walnut conference tables and executive chairs. Two rows of institutional folding chairs at the waist of the room are reserved for the wire-service reporters and the local beat men. The NBA lottery has not yet been swollen into a public relations extravaganza, so there are no television cameras on the scene, and only an occasional newspaper photographer. Three more rows of instant chairs are set up a respectful aisle behind the press: for friends, fans, and freebies. It is high noon, and most of the seats are vacant as, to a man, the assembly directs its attention to a hot buffet.

"Last year they had a roast beef dinner," says Saul Kent, a full-time college student and part-time ticket scalper. "I just walked in off the street, and a guy came up to me and said, 'Dinner is served.' It was delicious. Everything is open to the public, but hardly anybody knows about it. I tell all my friends, but they don't believe me. The whole thing is ridiculous."

The democracy fostered by scooping food from a common trough is total, and a twelve-year-old nephew of one of the Plaza's waiters sidles up to Jack McMahon, the coach of the Chicago Zephyrs. The boy wears jeans and sneakers, and he spews half-munched bits of fried chicken as he talks. "Draft Billy Pickens," the boy says.

"Hmmm?" says McMahon as he casually samples an exotic beef entree.

"Draft Billy Pickens. He's six-ten from Stetson College. It's in Florida."

"Hmmmm . . ." McMahon mumbles while he piles his plate with egg rolls.

"I heard him play on the radio," the boy says. "I can get the Miami games if I go up on the roof. Pickens scored 31 points, and he sounded terrific. You should draft him."

McMahon shrugs and inspects the potato pudding.

Saul Kent sits at a table nibbling spareribs and reading the *New York Post*. McMahon sits down facing him.

"You from New York?" McMahon asks.

"Of course," says Kent.

"Is Warren Isaacs any good?"

"From Iona," says Kent. "A reasonably good college player, but he'll never make it in the pros."

"Hmmm!" says McMahon, impressed.

The remains of the buffet are wheeled away, and the tables are cleaned. The coaches, scouts, general managers, and peripheral club officials cover the tables with lists and with scratch pads. But there are no telephones and the classy ballroom is half empty. The short man in the fat gray suit is Maurice Podoloff, the commissioner of the league. Podoloff is 4'11" and a round 150 pounds. He is partially obscured by the dais, and the chart looms far above his head; but the commissioner speaks briskly into the microphone: "This is the National Basketball Association's collegiate draft for 1962. Picking first is Chicago."

Jack McMahon doesn't hesitate. "Billy McGill," he says. "From Utah."

"The Chicago Zephyrs draft Billy McGill," repeats Podoloff. "From Utah."

The sportswriters trade knowing winks and glances. Billy "The Hill" McGill led the country in scoring with 38.8 ppg, most of them coming on a seemingly unstoppable jump hook. But McGill will have a pedestrian three-year career in the NBA before becoming an ABA gypsy.

"Drafting second is St. Louis."

The Hawks pick Zelmo Beaty from Prairie View A & M in Texas, and once more the writers cluck with approval. Beaty may have played in the "sticks," but the numbers and the eyewitnesses say he can't miss.

The hometown Knicks have the next choice, and the writers peer at coach Eddie Donovan. "Paul Hogue from Cincinnati," says Donovan.

"I knew it!" one of the writers yelps.

"Who else but the Knicks would draft a center who wears glasses?" says another.

"They blew it again," a third snickers.

In quick succession, Detroit picks Dave DeBusschere, Syracuse names Len Chappel, Cincinnati exercises its territorial rights and tabs Jerry Lucas, San Francisco selects Wayne Hightower, and Los Angeles gets Gene Wiley. Five days before the draft, the Boston Celtics captured their fourth consecutive NBA championship, and Red Auerbach has the last pick in every round. Auerbach calmly regards his cigar, while the writers lean forward and lick their pencils. "John Havlicek," Auerbach says with a slow smile. "From Ohio State."

The sportswriters nod at one another like the pigeons sitting in the chemical sunshine outside on the windowsills. "Of course," they chorus. "Of course," they coo.

In the bleachers, the waiter's nephew turns to his neighbor, the ticket scalper. "John Half-a-What?" the boy asks. "I never heard him before."

"I know him," says Kent. "Auerbach did it again. Havlicek's the greatest."

"But is he any good?" the boy asks. "Is he better than Billy Pickens?"

"Warren Isaacs is better than Billy Pickens," says Kent. "I get the Miami games, too. It didn't sound as though Pickens could go left. . . . But Havlicek can do everything. He can run, pass, score, rebound, and play defense. He's got heart. He's got two hearts."

On the sixth round the Knicks choose Warren Isaacs. Kent and McMahon seek each other's eyes and chuckle. The waiter's nephew turns to Kent's sudden laughter with a belligerent brow.

"The only thing Havlicek doesn't have is a position," Kent says to the boy. "But don't worry. Auerbach will invent one."

The '62–'63 Celtics were solid at every station: Bob Cousy, Sam Jones, and K. C. Jones split most of the guard time. The forwards were Tom Heinsohn, Tom Sanders, and Jungle Jim Loscutoff; all young, strong, and ferocious. Whatever relief Bill Russell required was provided by the veteran Clyde Lovellette. And Frank Ramsey was the Celtics' "sixth man."

Ramsey was a 6'3", 190-pound jackrabbit who played the pivot at the University of Kentucky (Cliff Hagan and Lou Tsioropoulos were the forwards). But Ramsey was well bred in every phase of the game, and he made up for his lack of size by playing with unlimited exuberance. As a pro Ramsey spent one-third of his playing time in the backcourt and the rest at forward. Jumbo forwards were the rage in the early 1960s, and Ramsey was often matched against 6'8", 225-pound Rudy LaRusso, 6'8", 220-pound Bailey Howell, and even 6'11", 250-pound Nate Thurmond. But Ramsey carried a fire around the court, and all the other players had to run like blazes to keep from getting burned.

Ramsey was also a notorious streak shooter. Yet he could find ways to score even when his shot was stricken, and he made a science of drawing fouls. . . . Ramsey is working the base line against Jack Twyman and the Cincinnati Royals as the Celtics try to beat the third-quarter buzzer with a score. Twyman leans his shoulder into Ramsey and forces him into the middle, where 6'8", 255-pound Wayne Embry prowls the foul lane. . . . Ramsey obligingly dribbles toward the big man's lair, but after two steps he spins back to the base line. Twyman stands his ground and uses his left forearm to fend off Ramsey's flashing left elbow. Ramsey leans forward, and their shoulders thwack. Then Ramsey hooks Twyman's left arm and falls backward, pulling his surprised defender down on top of him. On his way to the floor, Ramsey uncorks an off-balance sidearm desperado that grabs the backboard and plunks through the hoop. A foul is called on Twyman, and Ramsey gets up, dusts off his pants, and easily completes the 3-point play. . . .

Ramsey started for the Celtics only in dire emergencies and rarely played more than twenty-five minutes a game. "Ramsey was basketball's first great 'sixth man,'" says Tom Heinsohn. "He'd come off the bench and get three shots in twenty seconds and make something happen. Ramsey was unbelievable in the clutch. He played all the important minutes and he was always out there at the end of a close ball game."

The '62–'63 campaign was Ramsey's eighth as a pro and Havlicek's first. At age thirty-two, Ramsey's skills were undiminished, but he was increasingly susceptible to pulled leg muscles. Ramsey spent many private hours tutoring and grooming his replacement, and a comparison is inevitable: Ramsey was always the superior shooter, and he was also more creative with the ball. The rookie Havlicek had an iron-wristed jump shot, and his poor shooting was a mainline team joke. But the 6'5", 205-pound Havlicek was stronger, more effective without the ball, and he played with even more vitality than Ramsey. The '62–'63 season was ostensibly Cousy's last, and his retirement swing around the league was celebrated with packed houses, gifts, trophies, and speeches in appreciation. The Celtics capped Cousy's career by bopping Los Angeles in 6 games and notching their fifth consecutive title.

Ramsey's legs were a constant problem the following season, and he was often ineffective for the first time in his career. Havlicek's jumper remained profoundly unaesthetic, but somehow his shots began to fall. Hondo motored his way to 19.9 ppg and perpetuated the "sixth man" tradition in grand style. Sam Jones assumed full leadership in the Celtics' backcourt, and Cousy's departure was hardly noticed. The Celtics ran their string of championships to six by whipping San Francisco in 5 games.

The Celtics continued to rule the league until Russell finally retired in 1969. In his place, the woeful '69–'70 Celtics offered 6'9" Rich Johnson, who could run and jump; 6'8" Jim ("Bad News") Barnes, who was strong and ornery; and 7' Henry Finkel, who was smart. "All three of them put together didn't make half of Bill Russell," moaned coach Tom Heinsohn. The Celtics' brain trust decided to try to compensate for the gaping hole in the middle of the team by making Havlicek a starting forward. Havlicek remained in the Celtics' starting-and-finishing lineup for another nine years. Sometimes he played guard, but most often Havlicek cloned the "sixth man" into a "small forward" and transfigured the shape of the game.

NBA guards are certainly the fastest players in the league, and every one of them is active on the fast break. Yet a theoretical 48-minute guard runs only 5.2 miles a game, mostly from foul line to foul line. The forwards and centers rebound both baskets, run base line to base line, and cover 6.8 miles a game. But centers sometimes weigh 300 pounds and wear size 21 sneakers, and they are seldom fleet of feet. This means that the basic three-on-two fast-break overload must be created by a forward. By a "small forward" or "running forward." By an overgrown guard who may have trouble dribbling in a crowd but who can always help alleviate full-court pressure and trigger a fast break. By a strong, well-balanced athlete and a marathon runner in the Captain Hondo mold.

There's a basketball evergreen which postulates that "a good big man is better than a good little man." So above all, a small forward must always perform with intensity and intelligence. . . . Boston is playing San Antonio, and Havlicek is being engaged on defense by 6'9½" Larry Kenon, an outstanding offensive rebounder. Havlicek and Kenon play tag along the end line until one of the Spurs' guards launches a 25-foot shot. Havlicek immediately turns, sandbags Kenon to a halt, and then races downcourt. . . . Kenon has his eye on the ball and his mind on an offensive rebound and an easy hoop. So Kenon ignores Havlicek and plunges to the boards. . . . The shot is short, and Dave Cowens plucks the rebound and flips a full-court pass to Havlicek for a breakaway right-handed lay-up. . . .

Small forwards usually come in three distinct sizes: 6'4"—Mike Riordan and Mike Newlin; 6'5"—Bill Bradley, Junior Bridgeman, Bobby Dandridge, John Drew, Lou Hudson, Billy Knight, Jim McMillian, Bobby ("Bingo") Smith and Nate Williams; and 6'6"—Johnny Johnson, Bobby Gross, Scott Wedman, and Jamaal Wilkes. The propagation of small forwards in recent years has blasted the running game into overdrive. But small forwards are also accomplished passers and spot shooters who are invaluable members of deliberate ball clubs as well. Back-to-back bombs by a small forward compel a bigger man to come away from the basket and play tighter defense. And a zone defense is gutted whenever a big man is chasing after a small forward, since it becomes impossible to double-team a penetrating guard.

Jim McMillian is admittedly poor at driving to the basket, and when he goes one-on-one, he often goes nowhere. McMillian needs assistance to find a shot, but he has a deadeye from 20 feet out along either base line. In the middle 1970s, McMillian's savvy and quickness were the mainsprings of the Knicks' pattern offense. . . . McMillian is in his favorite shooting gallery—20 feet from the basket on the right base line. But McMillian doesn't have the ball, and he's also being closely guarded by Mike Newlin. . . . McMillian slides closer to the base line as Knick teammate Jim Cleamons dribbles across the midcourt line. When Cleamons approaches the foul-line-extended, McMillian turns and runs parallel to the base line, away from the basketball. . . . Newlin matches strides with McMillian until they reach the near margin of the foul lane, where the Knicks' Lonnie Shelton and Toby Knight are fused into a double pick. There's room for only one along the end line, so McMillian hits Newlin with a forearm and bounces him off Shelton's brawny shoulder. . . . McMillian finds himself wide open on the nether side of the double pick, but walled off from Cleamons and the ball. . . . The defense adjusts, and Knight's man scrambles over to cover McMillian. . . . "Jimmy Mack" now makes an abrupt about-face and retraces his steps back along the base line toward the ball. . . . Shelton has also spun around, and McMillian bangs his new defender into Shelton's other shoulder. . . . McMillian ends up exactly where he started; but this time he's all alone, and he easily changes Cleamons' pass into 2 points. . . . "In order for me to be effective on offense," says McMillian, "I have to get the ball coming off a pick. This makes it possible for me to force the defense into a lot of switches that my teammates can cash in. So my game depends on timing, discipline, and constant motion. I see myself as a supportive type of player. Small forwards are rarely superstars." A box score usually communicates very little about the complexion of a ball game. However, if a small forward on a pattern ball club scores 20 points, chances are his team has executed its plays, moved the ball well, and won the game.

With the rapid ascendancy of the small forward, Frank Ramsey's demonstration of the "sixth man" was amended to include fire-handed guards like Henry Bibby with New York, Flynn ("Instant Points") Robinson with Milwaukee, Dick Barnett with Syracuse and Los Angeles, Freddie ("Downtown") Brown with Seattle, and Lloyd Free with Philadelphia. In most cases, however, today's "sixth man" is a small forward with offensive dynamite, whose playing time is abbreviated by inexperience, lousy defense, a short attention span, too much mileage on his legs, or too much oil in his ego.

"Cazzie Russell was a great 'sixth man' for the Knicks," says Tom Heinsohn. "Cazzie could come in and change the entire flow of a ball game. But the Knicks didn't think Cazzie's role was all that important, and they didn't give him enough strokes. Cazzie wanted to start, and he began to sulk and rebel. Cazzie helped the Knicks win a championship in 1970, but he was very unhappy in New York. Eventually he was traded to Golden State and then on to Los Angeles, where he had similar problems. It's a classic syndrome. No matter how talented a player may be, he only hurts himself if he can't accept his role. And whichever way you get down to it, the willingness has to come from within."

SMALL FORWARDS

	BALL HANDLING	PASSING	SPEED	CREATING OWN SHOT	SPOT SHOOTING	SHOT SELECTION	SCORING	EFFECTIVENESS W/O BALL	DEFENSIVE POSITION	DEFENSIVE ANTICIPATION	REBOUNDING	STRENGTH	CONSISTENCY	VERSATILITY	DURABILITY	TOTAL
John Havlicek	3	4	3	3	4	4	4	4	3	4	2	3	4	4	4	53
Frank Ramsey	4	2	4	4	3	4	4	4	3	3	2	3	4	4	3	51
Bill Bradley	4	4	2	1	4	4	3	4	4	4	2	3	4	4	4	51
Bob Gross	2	3	3	2	4	4	2	4	4	4	4	3	4	3	4	50
Scott Wedman	4	2	3	3	4	4	3	3	4	3	3	3	4	4	4	50
Billy Knight	4	2	3	4	4	4	4	3	3	3	2	3	4	3	4	50
Jamaal Wilkes	2	1	3	3	4	3	3	3	4	3	4	3	3	3	4	46
Jim McMillian	2	4	2	2	4	4	3	4	3	3	3	4	3	2	3	46
Bob Dandridge	3	2	3	4	4	3	4	2	3	3	3	3	3	2	4	46
Adrian Dantley	3	1	3	4	3	3	4	2	3	3	3	4	3	2	4	45
John Drew	3	2	4	3	3	3	4	2	2	2	4	3	3	3	4	45
Junior Bridgeman	3	2	3	4	3	3	3	2	3	2	4	4	2	3	4	45
Nate Williams	2	2	2	3	4	3	3	2	2	2	3	4	3	3	4	42
John Johnson	3	2	3	3	4	3	3	3	2	2	2	2	3	3	4	42
Bingo Smith	2	2	2	2	4	3	3	4	3	2	2	2	3	2	4	40

LEGEND
4 = outstanding   3 = good   2 = average   1 = poor

10
THE LITTLE BIG MEN

They used to be called hatchet men. The blunt edges of their talents hewed out rebounds, picks, defense, and the kind of selective brutality essential to any contact sport. Virtually all the old-time hatchet men were forwards: 6'5", 240-pound Ed Sadowski; 6'6", 245-pound Ed Kalafat; 6'5", 220-pound Bob Brannum; 6'7", 225-pound Alex Hannum; 6'5", 230-pound Jim Loscutoff; 6'8", 240-pound Jim Barnes; 6'8", 225-pound Bud Olsen; 6'6", 230-pound Dave Piontek; and 6'8", 225-pound Toby Kimball. . . . All except for the NBA's Original Dead End Kid, a brazen 6'2", 180-pound guard named Al McGuire.

Allie was Dick McGuire's younger brother, both of them reared in a gutter-tough Irish ghetto in Queens and later teammates at St. John's University and with the New York Knicks. Tricky Dick was an effervescent ball handler and passer. Allie inherited a junior's share of basketball talent but an unmatched gift for hustling. . . . "I can stop Bob Cousy," Allie boasted one day back in 1952. "I can hold Cousy without a basket." On the following evening the lustiest crowd of the season jammed Madison Square Garden and watched with amazement as Allie McGuire tackled Cousy to the floor the first six times The Houdini of the Hardwoods touched the ball. McGuire fouled out within three minutes, leaving Cousy with six-for-six from the free-throw line, but shotless and basketless from the field. . . . McGuire played four otherwise undistinguished years with New York and Detroit and then retired after '54–'55, the Season of the Clock. McGuire then accepted a position as freshman coach at Dartmouth. Then in 1957 he popped up in North Carolina as head coach of Belmont Abbey College; and for the next eight years he masterminded an impressive record of winning seasons, tournament titles, and body counts. Then, in 1965, McGuire embarked on a long and glorious career as coach of the Marquette University Warriors. "At Marquette," says Maurice Lucas, "McGuire would stand over us in practice wearing a three-piece suit and playing the ringmaster. Whenever two guys would start to rough it up, McGuire would come over, pull them apart, and say, 'If you wanna fight, fight me.' McGuire never picked a fight with me, though. He only fought the guards. He also said that if he walked into an alley and three guys came in after him, he'd always be the one who walked out. And that's exactly the way he wanted us to play."

While he was on the scene, McGuire dominated collegiate basketball with his caustic wit and the shrewd, abrasive game he preached. He was named Coach of the Year in 1971 and 1976, and his career climaxed with an emotional victory over Kentucky for the 1976 NCAA championship. McGuire is currently a basketball consultant for NBC-TV, and the shadow of his influence is gone from the college game. But McGuire's vicarious presence is still alive in the pros, through a rosterful of successful NBA performers who served their brawling apprenticeships at Marquette—Dean Meminger, Jim Chones, George Thompson, Bo Ellis, Lloyd Walton, Earl Tatum, Butch Lee, Larry McNeill, and Jerome Whitehead. Yet Allie McGuire's most enduring legacy to the NBA is 6'9", 235-pound Maurice Lucas. . . .

The Portland Trail Blazers and the Philadelphia 76ers are clashing in the second game of the 1977 NBA championship series. The Blazers have Bill Walton in the middle and Lloyd Neal and Lucas "upfront." Philadelphia counters with Darryl

Dawkins, George McGinnis, and the prodigious Julius Erving. The Doctor is paired with Neal, while McGinnis and Lucas smash each other from pit to pit. . . .

Dave Twardzik controls the ball, and the Blazers run a play designed to spring Neal for a straightaway jumper from his favorite spot at the top of the key. Lucas installs himself halfway up the foul lane, while Neal barrels up from the base line and aims Erving into Lucas's chest. . . . But The Doctor bumps Neal offstride, and there's unexpected daylight between Neal and Lucas. Erving is about to slip through unscathed when Lucas slides to his left and throws his shoulder into The Doctor's rib cage. . . . Neal moves sharply to the appointed position, taking McGinnis with him on the switch and leaving Erving to deal with Lucas. . . . Neal accepts a pass from Twardzik, turns, and pumps up a 20-foot shot. . . . Lucas carries a full 2 inches and 30 pounds on Erving, so the Blazers' forward immediately powers to the basket. The Doctor responds by moving his own mortal body directly across Lucas's path in a valiant attempt to "box out" the bigger man and seal him from the offensive boards. But Lucas simply thumps a forearm into the small of Erving's back and shoves him off the road. . . . Neal's shot misses, and Lucas engulfs the rebound and stuffs it back through the hoop. . . .

But the caliber of play in the league is extraordinary, and there is a stringent eleven-man roster. So besides the strong-arm work, Lucas is expected to board, defend, set picks, and shoot in streaks. Lucas was trained and honed by a street fighter. He is a hit man with a talent.

The hatchet man is dead. Long live The Enforcer.

Around the NBA, the polite form of Enforcer is power forward or strong forward, and besides Lucas, the pretenders to greatness are legion—George McGinnis, Leon Douglas, Tim Bassett, Lonnie Shelton, Bill Robinzine, Jim Brewer, Jack Sikma, Mark Olberding, and Paul Silas. In fact, until they obtained McGinnis in 1978, the only team in the league which habitually played without a power forward was the Denver Nuggets, the NBA's speed maniacs.

Most of a power forward's duties are fulfilled away from the ball, including the setting of picks. A pick is an exercise in interference that's just as important to a deliberate offense as an accurate jump shot. The picker plants himself strategically and tries to block the path of the defender. A pick on the strong side (the ball side) is usually calculated to free a good shooter and create an immediate shot. Weak-side picks are aimed at forcing the defense into disadvantageous switches. In the NBA most of the strong-side picks are galvanized by centers. "You always knew where Wilt's picks were," says Steve Patterson, a power forward miscast as a center in the pros. "Same thing with Jabbar's picks, Thurmond's, and all the rest of the big centers. But the weak-side picks are mostly set by power forwards, especially in pattern offenses. A forward covers more ground than a center, and you're usually moving backwards into a weak-side pick, so you can really get racked up. Picks set by forwards make you hear footsteps all over the court and definitely scatter your concentration."

Setting picks is a serious undertaking, and there have always been pick specialists in the NBA: Vern Mikkelsen, Jack Coleman, John Kerr, Art Spoelstra, Charlie Share, Wayne Embry, Willis Reed, Dave Cowens, and Dave DeBusschere— players with the knack of rippling their bodies just before the moment of impact. "The effect," says Steve Patterson, "is like getting slammed with a shovel. A good pick can untie your shoelaces and loosen your fillings."

But John Havlicek warns that even the most punishing pick must be used correctly. "You should actually rub shoulders with your teammate as he's setting the pick," says Hondo. "Then there's no way the defensive man can get through without committing an obvious foul."

A legal pick is supposed to be perfectly stationary, and the "pickee" allowed room to change direction and avoid the contact. But that's only theory, and a good pick is far too valuable to be curtailed by mere legality. "All the good players set moving picks," says Chet Walker, a perennial All-Star with the Chicago Bulls. "Some guys just do it better than others. The refs really don't have a chance on the call unless they're specifically looking for it. If you can move on the pick, you can nail your man every time. All you have to do is make it look like you're moving only because the defensive man has run into you. If the officials see anything, they just see the contact. Then they either have to guess who initiated it or ignore it. Most of them let it go."

In addition to his picking game, a good power forward must be accomplished in the martial art of rebounding. Good defensive rebounding can deny an opposing team as many as fifteen extra shots every ball game—or up to 16½ fewer points per game. According to Bill Russell, who collared 21,620 career caroms, 95 percent of all rebounds are actually captured below the level of the rim. Yet most of the players in the NBA persist in believing that the best jumpers are always the best rebounders. The truth is that bounce and strength are important factors, but position and timing make the difference. . . . Paul Silas is a 6′6″, 220-pound power forward for the Seattle SuperSonics who has a Black Belt in Rebounding. The Sonics are entertaining the Philadelphia 76ers when, early in the third quarter, Silas is creamed by a moving pick and forced to switch on to 6′11″, 265-pound Darryl Dawkins. . . . A shot is quickly taken from the other side of the court, and Silas turns to box out the eager nineteen-year-old center. Dawkins gallops straight to the back-board and is almost within clawing distance of the rim. But Silas heads the rookie off at the pass, bangs his butt into Dawkins's thighs, slams a shoulder into his chest, and blasts the rookie to attention. . . . The shot misses, and the ball sails in their direction; but the big man is on his heels, and Silas barely has to leave the ground to nab the rebound. . . .

"It's very hard to teach NBA players to box out," says Tom Sanders, the learned ex-coach of the Boston Celtics. "They're all programmed to release to the ball and start jumping as soon as the shot goes up. The technique of boxing out is similar to pass blocking in football. The man has to get past you to get to the ball. So the longer you can wait, the more of him you can get when you hit him." But in the topsy-turvy world of the NBA there are also times when boxing out is undesirable. "If your opponent is much stronger than you," says Sanders, "you create the contact when you box him out, and you allow him to utilize his strength. Sometimes it's better just to rely on your quickness to get to the rebound. It all depends on the match-ups."

Some power forwards like Dave DeBusschere, E. C. Coleman, and Corky Calhoun were out-and-out defensive specialists. But all power forwards must be very active in the man-to-zone defenses played in the NBA. On the strong side, a power forward plays aggressive defense in his man's face. The man-to-man pressure is always relaxed on the weak side, permitting the forwards to drift over and help clog the middle. "If you want to help out on defense and not get burned yourself," says Phil Jackson, "then you have to know where the ball is and where your man is. The problem is that you can never turn your head away from your man, and on the weak side you're usually too far away to feel where he is. So what you have to do is open your body and your line of sight. You have to look between your man and the ball until you're aware of them both. It's a matter of instinct, peripheral vision, anticipation, and balance."

If power forwards do most of their work without the ball, they must also be capable of scoring enough points to warrant honest defensive attention. Since most power forwards are mediocre shooters, they have to develop pet moves and favorite spots: Tim Bassett looks for a lefty hook, and Leon Douglas likes to spin to his left for a 10-foot jumpie. Offensive rebounds are also easy shots that a power forward can always generate for himself. . . . Paul Silas takes a pass from Fred Brown and finds himself in the clear only a step beyond the foul line. But Silas ignores the free shot, returns the ball to the sharpshooting Brown, and begins his journey to the offensive boards. . . . Silas zeroes in along the base line, then to avoid being boxed out, he runs an unexpected "banana" route that takes him out of bounds. Silas finally arrives in the attack zone from underneath the basket. . . . Silas now has the inside rebounding position, and he pushes backward to get a better angle as Brown lofts a jumper from the far corner. . . . The shot is short, and Silas lunges off the ground and grabs the rebound. Then he climbs back up to the basket and hits on a twisting lay-up. . . .

"It's all a question of logic," says Tom Heinsohn, who coached Silas at Boston. "Silas isn't a good outside shooter, but even if he makes six of ten shots, he still hurts his ball club. If Silas is shooting from the outside, that means he's in poor position for four rebounds. That also means that his center is getting double-teamed under the boards and that a guard has to crash and rebound or else all four missed shots might as well be conceded to the defense. If the crashing guard gets one of the four rebounds, then the team's total potential for Silas's ten shots is 14 points. But if a good shooter takes ten shots and makes the same six, Silas will most likely get two of the four rebounds. The potential for the same ten shots is now 16 points."

Most coaches describe a power forward's responsibilities in terms of "sacrifice," but Bill Fitch disagrees. "Rebounding, picking and playing defense are all vital ingredients in a ball game." says Fitch. "Somebody has to do the country work. But to call what's necessary a sacrifice. . . . Well, that only shows that even the NBA is a victim of the American way of life."

Yet the role of power forward is indeed a difficult one, and a ballplayer must sometimes lose touch with his essence in the doing. . . . There's just 4:25 remaining in the second game of the 1977 championship play-offs, and Philadelphia is roasting the Trail Blazers by 20 points. . . . As Bob Gross and Darryl Dawkins contest a rebound, they collide and are sent spilling to the floor. Dawkins is generally regarded as the strongest player in the league, and he sprawls over and violently rips the ball away from Gross. Both men immediately jump to their feet and square off. Then Doug Collins, a Sixers' guard, suddenly grabs Gross from behind and holds him for Dawkins to clobber. Dawkins obliges with a savage left hook that misses Gross and clips Collins in the eye. . . . Maurice Lucas now enters the fracas by charging Dawkins and punching the rookie in the back of the neck. Dawkins spins around, and the two behemoths face each other with willing, whirling fists. Lucas is perceptibly more anxious than the rookie, and he taunts Dawkins with street-corner abuse. The youngster leans away slightly. But fists are cocked for another meaningless moment until the referees thrust their invulnerable gray shirts between two players. . . .

For the remainder of the series Lucas plays like a tiger, Dawkins plays like a kitten, and the Blazers win the next four games and the championship. . . . But even with a championship ring on his finger, the rude confrontation with Dawkins disturbed Lucas for months. "I didn't like what happened out there," Lucas later told sportswriter Marty Bell. "I really wasn't impressed with myself. I've thought about it a lot, and I've asked myself if it was all really necessary. But I still don't know why I did it. All I know is that wasn't really me!"

Yet despite the brutalizing demands of the power forward position, it can be played with finesse and with psychic integrity. . . . Phil Jackson is a slim 6'8", 220-pounder and a twelve-year veteran. Jackson plays with apparent inconsistency, with a notable predilection for angles, elbows, and mad flappings, and with a gawky freneticism. "Phil doesn't look very pretty," says ex-teammate Willis Reed, "but he knows what he's doing out there. He works hard without the ball, and he's a great influence on everybody. Phil can even score if he has to. When the Knicks won the championship in 1973, Phil averaged double figures coming off the bench. He's also stronger than he looks, and he was my backup center in 1967. But the single most important thing that Phil always does is to change the flow of a ball game as soon as he steps on the court. Not too many ballplayers have the ability to affect a ball game as dramatically as he does."

At 6'9" and 212 pounds, Bobby Jones seems frail and hunched even when compared to Jackson. Yet many players and coaches swear that Jones in his prime was the finest power forward in the game. . . . The Denver Nuggets and the Golden State Warriors are locked in a barbarous ball game. During one time-out, Denver coach Larry Brown accuses referee Ed Rush of letting the game get out of hand. . . . Denver guard Bobby Wilkerson dribbles across the time line early in the fourth quarter, badgered by the hand checking of Charles Dudley. When Wilkerson reaches the top of the key, he is kneed in the thigh. The Denver guard retaliates by passing the ball and then slashing Dudley's rib cage with an elbow. . . . Beneath the basket, Nugget forward Darnell Hillman hooks Warrior center Robert Parish by the arm and jerks him out of position. Parish answers by chopping Hillman on the shoulder. . . . Away from the ball, Denver's David Thompson is skidding on the floor after being bowled over by Phil Smith. . . . And in the far corner, Golden State's Nate Williams is treating Bobby Jones with minimal respect, holding and tripping him in one motion. . . . Jones is staggered, but he catches his balance and swivels to the basket. Williams is spun around and screwed into the ground, while Jones accepts a pass for a running stuff shot. . . .

"Bobby Jones doesn't punch, shove, or push," says Larry Brown. "He won't make contact unless he has to. Yet Bobby consistently gets the job done against bigger and stronger players. Bobby always plays tough on defense, and he boxes out well so his teammates can release to the boards. On defense, he covers up for his teammates' mistakes, and he makes them all better players. Bobby is constantly on the move, and he doesn't have to hog the ball to score. Look for Bobby to make the pass that starts a play, not the pass that ends it. Watching Bobby Jones on the basketball court is like watching an honest man in a liars' poker game."

Power forwards (and small forwards) concentrate on the more esoteric aspects of the game, but every team also requires a forward whose full-time specialty is scoring points. This scoring forward position has always showcased the most individualistic talent in the game. Some rely on outside shooting—Kenny Sears, George Yardley, Willie Naulls, Jack Marin, Rudy Tomjanovich, and Campy Russell. Some depend on strength and quick moves to the basket—Bob Pettit, Elgin Baylor, Billy Cunningham, John Shumate, and 6'5" Adrian Dantley, a pint-sized pivot man. Some are runners and gliders—Larry Kenon, Walter Davis, Marques Johnson, and Julius Erving.

Scoring forwards must obviously score points to be useful, but they also tend to force their own individual will upon a ball game. A scoring forward will often decide to shoot the very next time he touches the ball and hit or miss, forced shots can easily destroy a team's offensive rhythm. . . . The recently retired Bob Love is an All-Star example of a scoring forward who moved with the flow. "To be truly effective on offense," says Love, "a scoring forward has to wear his man down. He has to bring him inside and then bring him outside. Move him from one half of the court to the other. I really wasn't strong enough to fight aggressive defensive pressure. So if someone tried to keep me from going right, then I'd go left. If I got bumped, then I'd change direction and go another way. But I always kept moving. Sooner or later my man would get tired, and I had all the open shots I could use."

Scoring forwards can also present unusual problems for a defense if they can handle the ball and are quick enough to penetrate. A penetrating forward like 6'7", 220-pound Rick Barry can outmaneuver most defensive forwards and almost single-handedly destroy a zone defense. . . . The Warriors are playing the Lakers, and Rick Barry has deftly dribbled around his man and is cruising along the base line on his way to the basket. With the Lakers in a two-two-one funnel zone there's nobody to support Barry's erstwhile defender but the Lakers' center, Kareem Abdul-Jabbar. The big man must honor Barry's offense, so he moves over to block the basket and darken the sky. . . . But Clifford Ray, the Warriors' center, has been playing with Barry for four years, and he cuts behind Abdul-Jabbar and toward the basket. Barry freezes Abdul-Jabbar's sneakers with a nifty head fake. Ray then picks up Barry's bounce pass and throws down a gleeful dunker. . . .

There are a number of roles a forward can assume, and a player's game is bound to suffer is he's at all confused about his function. . . . Elvin Hayes was publicly upset with his team-mates after the Washington Bullets were eliminated by the Houston Rockets in the 1977 Eastern Conference play-offs. "The only reason we lost," said Hayes, "was because our center had a terrible series." The remark was widely interpreted as being a gibe at Wes Unseld, a 6'7½", 255-pound bulwark rebounder, passer, and picker. But Unseld scoffed at Hayes's accusation. "It may be that the Bullets' center had a bad series," said Unseld. "Hayes would know that better than anybody else because *he* is the Bullets' center."

The confusion is totally understandable since Hayes usually defends against forwards and plays a unique variation of the center position on offense. . . . Hayes receives a pass deep in the pivot with his back to the basket. He fakes a haphazard pass to a cutting guard. Then he takes two earnest dribbles away from the basket, spins sharply to his right, and releases a fadeaway jumper that hits nothing but cotton. By the time he lands Hayes is nearly 25 feet from the basket. . . .

If there are small forwards, power forwards, defensive forwards, scoring forwards, and penetrating forwards, then Elvin Hayes is the only backwards-forward in the NBA.

FORWARDS

	BALL HANDLING	PASSING	SPEED	CREATING OWN SHOT	SPOT SHOOTING	SHOT SELECTION	SCORING	EFFECTIVENESS W/O BALL	DEFENSIVE POSITION	DEFENSIVE ANTICIPATION	STRENGTH	OFFENSIVE REBOUNDING	DEFENSIVE REBOUNDING	CONSISTENCY	VERSATILITY	DURABILITY	TOTAL
Dave DeBusschere	3	3	2	3	3	4	3	4	4	4	3	4	4	4	4	4	56
Elgin Baylor	3	4	2	4	3	3	4	3	3	2	4	4	4	4	4	4	55
Julius Erving	4	3	4	4	3	3	4	2	1	4	4	3	4	3	4	4	54
Rick Barry	4	4	3	4	4	4	4	4	4	4	2	2	1	3	3	4	54
Bob Pettit	2	3	2	3	4	4	4	3	3	2	4	4	4	4	4	4	54
Dolph Schayes	3	3	2	3	3	4	4	3	3	2	4	4	4	4	4	4	54
Billy Cunningham	3	3	3	4	3	3	4	3	3	2	3	4	4	4	4	3	53
Bobby Jones	3	4	4	1	3	3	3	4	4	4	3	3	3	4	3	4	53
Lonnie Shelton	3	2	4	3	3	3	3	3	3	4	4	4	4	2	3	4	52
E. C. Coleman	2	2	3	2	3	4	2	4	4	4	4	3	3	4	3	4	51
George McGinnis	3	3	4	3	2	2	4	3	2	4	4	4	4	2	3	4	51
Maurice Lucas	2	2	2	3	3	3	3	3	4	2	4	4	4	3	3	4	50
Paul Silas	2	3	2	2	1	4	2	4	4	4	4	4	4	3	2	4	49
Tom Heinsohn	2	2	2	3	4	3	4	4	3	2	4	3	4	3	4	4	49
Larry Kenon	3	2	4	3	3	3	4	2	2	3	3	4	4	2	3	4	49
Truck Robinson	2	1	4	3	3	3	4	2	2	3	4	4	4	3	2	4	48
Jim Brewer	2	2	4	2	2	3	2	3	4	4	4	3	3	3	3	4	48
Elvin Hayes	2	1	4	4	3	2	4	2	3	3	4	4	4	2	2	4	48
Vern Mikkelsen	2	2	1	2	2	4	3	4	3	1	4	4	4	4	3	4	47
Campy Russell	4	2	3	4	4	3	4	2	2	2	2	2	3	3	2	4	46
Kermit Washington	1	2	3	2	3	3	3	3	2	4	4	4	4	3	3	3	45
Sidney Wicks	3	3	4	4	3	3	3	2	2	2	3	3	3	2	2	3	45
Rudy Tomjanovich	2	2	2	2	4	4	4	3	3	2	3	3	2	3	2	4	45
Leon Douglas	1	2	2	3	2	2	2	3	3	2	4	4	3	3	3	4	43
Spencer Haywood	2	1	4	4	3	2	3	2	2	2	2	4	3	2	3	3	42

LEGEND
4 = outstanding   3 = good   2 = average   1 = poor

11

THE BIG MEN

When Dr. James Naismith nailed a peach basket to the wall of the Springfield Armory YMCA in December of 1891 and then tossed a soccer ball to his physical education class, it was hard to tell the offense from the defense, the guards from the forwards from the centers. With nine players on a side, it didn't seem to make much difference. But legend holds that Lyman W. Archibald, the tallest player for the "shirts," tallied the only basket in that historic contest, a 25-foot running two-hander. . . . During the next few years the teams were trimmed to five players, and lines were painted on the floor. Then, just before the turn of the century, Dr. Naismith cut a hole in the bottom of the peach basket. The game developed quickly, but tall players were valued only for rebounding and for contesting the jump ball that succeeded every basket. The centers ranged from 6'2" to 6'5", and girth and strength were far more important than height.

The game was savage in the early 1920s, and the barnstorming pros often played inside huge wire cages built to protect the courtside fans. Defense began with the precept that "the head is part of the ball." The standard offense was a "figure eight," and everybody handled the ball in a continuous weave: The aim was to lull the defense and then change direction with a "give-and-go." The standing guard was also common at the time: a player who was stationed at the foul line and never moved downcourt, not even when his own team had the ball. No player, whatever his size or position, ever took anything but a right-handed lay-up, a left-handed lay-up, or a set shot.

The Original Celtics were the best and most innovative of the early pro teams. One night in Miami, Florida, the Celtics ran up an early 30–1 lead and took the opportunity to rehearse some new plays. But the opponents' standing guard kept interfering with the Celtics' passing game until 6'5" Henry ("Dutch") Dehnert came up with a startling suggestion. "I volunteered to stay in front of the standing guard with my back to the basket," said Dehnert, "so that he couldn't break up our passes. We tried it a few times, and it worked. My teammates would pass to me, and I would give it right back to them. Then in an effort to bat the ball out of my hand, the standing guard moved around to my right side. All I had to do was turn to my left, take one step, and lay the ball in. Of course, we didn't know it at the time, but this was the first pivot play."

The Celtics incorporated the pivot man into their regular offense, and it didn't take long to realize that the closer he played to the basket, the more easy shots he got. Dehnert was succeeded in the pivot by Horace ("Horse") Haggerty and Joe Lapchick, and in the early 1930s it even became fashionable to use a double pivot. But one fatal drawback of having two big men squatting on opposite sides of the foul lane was the clotting of a team's offense, and the style was quickly abandoned. Yet the advantages of a single pivot man were undeniable: scores of "cheap" baskets, offensive rebounds, and foul shots.

In the mid-1940s the big men took over the game. College basketball was dominated by 6'10", 265-pound George Mikan of De Paul, the country's leading scorer, and also by a talented 7-footer named Bob ("Foothills") Kurland, who led Oklahoma

A&M to consectuive NCAA titles in 1945 and 1946. Kurland loved to pass, pick, and play defense, and his favorite ploy was to station himself directly under the basket and block shots like a hockey goalie. It was primarily because of Kurland that the NCAA outlawed defensive goaltending in 1945. Kurland and Mikan faced each other several times as collegians with neither man playing to an advantage. Then, in a highly publicized Red Cross benefit game held in Madison Square Garden in March 1945, Kurland outscored Mikan, 14–9, and Oklahoma A&M defeated De Paul, 52–44. A few months later Kurland spurned the pros to accept a well-paying job with Phillips Petroleum, his most significant obligation being to play for the company basketball team—The Phillips Oilers, aka The 66ers. Kurland was technically still an amateur, and he paced the 1948 USA Olympic basketball team to a gold medal in London.

In the meantime, hardly anybody cared what was going on in the Basketball Association of America: Red Auerbach's '46–'47 Washington Capitols were a fast, good-shooting ball club. Auerbach's main problem was that his pivot man—6'8", 220-pound John Mahnken from Georgetown—was an atrocious shooter. Mahnken was also a fine picker and an outstanding passer, skills rarely exercised by contemporary pivot men. Auerbach's solution was to move his pivot man to a "high post" on the foul line. This left the middle open for cutters and brought everybody into Mahnken's picking and passing range. But nobody noticed Auerbach's tinkering because George Mikan was establishing the pivot man as an overwhelming offensive force in professional basketball.

In an age where 75 points was a high number for a pro team to score, Mikan topped his career with 28.4 ppg in '50–'51 and with a one-game mark of 61 points in 1952. The bespectacled Mikan led the NBL in scoring twice and the NBA three times. His moves around the basket were forceful, smooth, and virtually unstoppable. "Nobody ever made it easy for George," says Jumping Jim Pollard, Mikan's teammate in the golden years of the Minneapolis Lakers. "George earned every one of his baskets, and he also got fifteen rebounds a game. Once he positioned himself under the basket, he was tough to push out. For rival players, it was like trying to move the Statue of Liberty. The rules makers tried to hinder George by widening the three-second lane from six feet to ten feet and then to twelve feet. But all that did was give George more room to maneuver and beat his man."

Up until Bill Russell, a center's chief function was to score points, and the young NBA didn't bother to keep rebounding statistics until 1950. And as coaches observed the apparent invincibility of the pivot man, the NBA soon abounded with "The Ersatz Mikans" (Larry Foust, Don Otten, Ray Felix, Alex Groza): "The One-Handed Stabber and Hooksters" (Ed Macauley, Bob Houbregs, Connie Simmons, John Kerr, Neil Johnston, Clyde Lovellette, Red Rocha, Joe Grabowski): "The Minuscule Two-Handed Setter" (6'5" Nat Clifton, who defensed Mikan better than anybody): and 6'9", 200-pound Arnie Risen, the original "Spider Man."

Then, in 1952, the world was alerted to Wilton Norman Chamberlain, only a sophomore at Philadelphia's Overbrook High School but already a gangling 6'10". During Chamberlain's matriculation at Overbrook, the team won 58 games and lost only 3. Young Wiltie averaged 36.9 ppg, even though he seldom played more than twenty minutes a game. He scored mostly on one-handers from both corners, two-handers from the key, and an assortment of dunks and scoops. "I once scored 60 points in ten minutes," says Wilt. "Against a team that was freezing the ball." But Chamberlain wasn't just the latest basketball goon; sometimes he dribbled behind his back, and sometimes he triggered a fast break. At Overbrook, Chamberlain also high-jumped 6'6", put the shot 47 feet, ran the 440 in 48.6 and the 880 in 1:58.6.

Chamberlain was wooed by 205 colleges, and he wound up at the University of Kansas on a combination basketball-and-track scholarship. The NCAA immediately launched an investigation into rumors of recruiting violations. Chamberlain averaged 30 points and 19 rebounds in his first varsity season, most of them coming despite double- and triple-teaming. Chamberlain was always a horrid foul shooter, and as a sophomore he would start his free throws a stride beyond the foul circle. . . . Chamberlain squeezes the ball in his right hand and shakes his legs loose. Then he takes a mincing high jumper's approach and bounces off the foul line. . . . He swoops like a prehistoric bird, then he reaches, and then he dunks the ball before his feet hit the ground. . . . Kansas's favorite inbounds play from under its own basket was a simple over-the-backboard pass and a "Dipper Dunk." But the NCAA quickly legislated both plays out of existence. Kansas went to the finals of the NCAA tournament in 1957 only to be beaten by North Carolina in a thrilling triple-overtime ball game.

Then Chamberlain suffered a painful groin in his junior year, and Kansas failed to qualify for postseason play. The NCAA was still sleuthing around the campus, and Chamberlain was frustrated, hassled, and bored. Since NBA teams were prohibited from drafting underclassmen, Chamberlain opted to spend his senior year playing with the Harlem Globetrotters.

When Chamberlain drew his first NBA breath in 1959, he was a full-grown 7'1¼" and 285 pounds. As a pro he was also a modern-day wonder—a pivot man who was brilliantly suited to the quickness of the 24-second game. Chamberlain easily led the league in scoring with 37.6 ppg as a rookie. . . . Tom Gola tosses a rainbow pass to Chamberlain deep in the pivot. As Chamberlain extends to receive the ball, Bill Russell slides forward and forces the big man to land a few feet farther from the basket. . . . Russell overplays Chamberlain's right, and the rookie starts to drub the ball against the floor, his massive shoulders rippling with fakes. . . . Russell alternately pushes and taps Chamberlain's base-line shoulder, but the big man is too strong and too quick to be confused. . . . Chamberlain stretches and wheels to his right, carrying Russell on his shoulder. . . . Russell makes a leaping swipe at the ball; then he jumps off and ducks away as Chamberlain crashes the ball through the hoop. . . .

During Chamberlain's thirteen-year NBA career he led the league in scoring seven times, rebounding eleven times, field goal percentage nine times, minutes played eight times, and assists once. Chamberlain is also the only player in NBA history with a career scoring mark of over 30 a game. . . . Wade ("Swede") Halbrook was a low-scoring 7'3" center with the old Syracuse Nationals who provided an unerring appraisal of Chamberlain's phenomenal point production. "If Wilt got 35 points," said Halbrook, "his team would lose by 5. If he got 45, they lost by 15. If he got 55, they lost by 25."

Wilt Chamberlain solidified the tradition of the Mikanesque pivot man, but he also proved that a high-scoring center offers no guarantee of success. Chamberlain won championships (in 1967 with Philadelphia and 1972 with Los Angeles) only when he drastically reduced his scoring (24.1 in 1967 and 14.8 in 1972). In fact, over the last twenty-three years, the NBA championship has been captured only three times by a team whose center averaged as much as 20 points a game: Philadelphia had Chamberlain in 1967, New York had Willis Reed (21.7) in 1970, and Milwaukee had Kareem Abdul-Jabbar (31.7) in 1970. A ball club will always reflect the character, talent, and mobility of its center, especially on offense, and there are several distinct disadvantages in playing a big man who must operate with his back to the basket.

In any sport, the defense has an edge in every clutch situation when even the peanut vendors know where the ball is headed. A high-scoring pivot man invites a sagging, collapsing zone defense—a strategy which still yields easy points to any hardworking big man, but which also keeps the rest of the team far away from the hoop.

An immobilized pivot man cannot effectively articulate with either a penetrating guard or a penetrating forward. Norm Van

Lier used to be the finest penetrating guard in the NBA, but since Artis Gilmore set up shot in "the hole," Van Lier has no place to go and no real function on offense. "It's a real shame," says Bill Fitch. "I know that Van Lier is very frustrated. But Gilmore is seven-two so that's just too bad for Van Lier." By constructing an entire offense around a pivot man, a ball club cancels out its own speed and quickness and chooses to rely on size, position, and strength.

Tom Heinsohn has coached and/or played on nine championship Celtic teams. "In my book," says Heinsohn, "anybody who averages 30 points a game is hurting his team. The more points you expect from one guy, the harder they are to deliver. The Lakers lose whenever Jabbar has an off night. I'd much rather have a big man getting 18 points a game and a forward averaging the other 12. Two players will give me the same 30 points much more consistently than one big guy in the middle. For an NBA offense to succeed night after night, it needs speed and flexibility."

The NBA's current offensive leviathans include 6'11", 250-pound Bob Lanier; 7'2", 255-pound Artis Gilmore; 7'2½", 228-pound Tom Burleson; 6'11", 230-pound Jim Chones; 6'11", 255-pound Swen Nater; and 6'10", 220-pound Moses Malone. But the field indubitably belongs to 7'2", 232-pound Kareem Abdul-Jabbar. "Having Jabbar on your side is a mixed blessing," says Joe Axelson, president and general manager of the Kansas City Kings. "But having Jabbar is also a definite curse. When Larry Costello coached Jabbar at Milwaukee, the Bucks used twenty-eight different plays just to get the ball into the pivot. Now, Jabbar can certainly do a lot of things with a basketball in his hands. There's no question about his ability. But when it comes right down to it, you're forced to live or die on a fifteen-foot skyhook. And if you don't go to him in the clutch, everybody thinks you're crazy."

Kareem Abdul-Jabbar can shoot, pass, rebound, dribble, block shots, set picks, and push people around. He is the ultimate basketball talent and a certified champion. During his enchanted youth, "Lew Alcindor" carried an aging, ailing Oscar Robertson, an inexperienced Bobby Dandridge, and a wild-driving Lucius Allen to an NBA championship. Since then, collapsing zone defenses have become much more sophisticated, and Abdul-Jabbar has taken his teams to four regular season divisional titles but nary another championship. "Because of the style of ball that Jabbar plays," says Bob Gross of the Portland Trail Blazers, "it's possible that he'll win another championship. But in my opinion, it's certainly not probable."

A high-scoring pivot man limits the offensive capabilities of his teammates, yet there are numerous ways for a center to score points without impeding the flow. . . . The Boston Celtics are in the midst of a fast break, but their three-on-two edge fails to yield a satisfactory shot, so Jo Jo White pulls the ball off to the side and waits. . . . The defense is hustling, and the Celtics are soon playing four-on-four. . . . Then Dave Cowens suddenly pops through the keyhole, roars down the lane, and takes a pass from White. . . . Cowens dribbles once and hits a lollipop jump shot over a helpless guard. . . . On the very next offensive sequence, the Celtics' break churns up a four-on-three advantage. Kevin Stacom misses a complicated lay-up, but Cowens arrives just in time to tip in the rebound. . . .

Centers can always run themselves into easy scoring opportunities because they trail the play and can see how the defense is deployed. On offense, a running center gets lay-ups when he fills the open lanes and easy jumpers when he fades to the unguarded areas. But not all NBA centers can run, and most of those who can simply don't want to. "Centers take a furious beating under both boards," says one anonymous big man. "That slows you down a lot. So does running from end to end. It's also a fact that running centers usually have short careers."

Clyde Lovellette was the first big man in the NBA who could shoot from 15–20 feet, and there have been a herd of good shooting centers ever since. Ed Macauley, Connie Simmons, Jim Krebs, Zelmo Beaty, Henry Finkel, Mel Counts, Bob Lanier, Dave Cowens, Billy Paultz, and Jim Chones all could score a big man's share of points without clogging the middle. Jerry Lucas and Bob McAdoo had the shooting range of guards. But running and shooting are not the only ways for a center to produce unobtrusive points: The Golden State Warriors won the NBA title in 1975 with a pair of horrible shooters sharing the center spot, Clifford Ray and George Johnson. The combo managed 11.3 "garbage" points a game by hustling and by synchronizing their movements with Rick Barry.

Through the years the NBA has also featured a solid string of superior passing centers—John Mahnken, John Kerr, George Mikan, Nat Clifton, Jerry Lucas, and Neal Walk. . . . Most of the St. Louis Hawks' offensive plays don't begin until Easy Ed Macauley receives a pass near the top of the key. Macauley pivots and faces the basket, waving the ball and keeping his shot a constant threat. Hawks' guard Jack McMahon is supposed to release to the near corner and pick for Med Park, a forward, but the defense moves a step ahead of the play. McMahon reacts without thinking: He fakes setting the pick, and then he slices to the basket against the defensive grain. . . . Macauley finds him with a quick-draw pass from the hip, and McMahon has a lay-up. . . .

The current roster of passing centers includes 6'9" Alvan Adams, 7'0" Tom Boerwinkle, 6'10" Sam Lacey, 6'10" Dennis Awtrey, and 7'0" Rich Kelley. But Bill Walton is easily the most versatile passing center in the league. . . . "Let me run it down for you," says the recently involuntarily retired Dean Meminger. "Walton can play inside and outside. He can score from the pivot when he has to. He also has great concentration and uncanny court sense. He knows exactly where everybody is and where they're going. His passes are always easy to handle. He plays with intelligence, and he's always in the ball game. But the main thing about Walton is that the Blazers' system has been molded to fit his individual talents. Maurice Lucas does all the muscle work, and Bob Gross does the running and cutting. Portland's front line is a wonderful blend of roles, and they can harmonize just as well on defense."

A center's contributions are important on offense, but they are the essence of defense. A big man's defensive tasks have always included rebounding, preventing easy baskets, and ruling the middle. Yet before Bill Russell, a big man was required only to block the shots of the opposing center. Russell's revolution moved the defensive emphasis away from guarding a man and toward attacking the ball. Russell turned lay-ups into jump shots, and he changed the blocked shot from an accident into an enduring art form. . . .

Wayne Rollins is a 7′1″, 245-pound rookie center for the Atlanta Hawks who's still learning his way around the league. The Hawks are playing the Knicks at the Omni, and midway through the second quarter, Bob McAdoo dribbles his way into a jump shot from the foul line. Rollins is guarding Spencer Haywood, but the rookie sniffs out the free man and attacks the shot. Rollins throws an overhand bolo punch and blasts the ball cleanly out of bounds. But the whistle blows anyway, and a foul is called on the rookie. . . . "The refs will always call a foul if you take a full-arm swing at the ball," says Nate Thurmond, the third-ranking career rebounder in the NBA. "They'll whistle you even if there's no contact. So a rookie has to adapt his game, or else he gets into constant foul trouble. The only acceptable way to block shots in the NBA is to go up and just flick your wrist and tap the ball away. That's exactly the way that Russell used to do it."

The tallest centers are not necessarily the best shot blockers. Most of the bigger men—like Bob Lanier, Artis Gilmore, Kent Benson, Tom Burleson, and Swen Nater—have to gather themselves before they jump and are very slow off the floor. In '77–'78, George Johnson of the New Jersey Nets was the NBA's leading shot blocker. Johnson was a slender 6'10" and an awesome leaper who averaged about one blocked shot for every nine minutes of playing time. But like most leapers, Johnson was too eager to leave his feet and was susceptible to fakes. Johnson has been battling chronic foul trouble throughout his career and can rarely be counted on for more than 25 effective minutes a ball game. Bill Walton was the NBA's top shot blocker in '76–'77, and if Walton lacks exceptional size and spring, he gets off the floor quickly and his timing is exemplary. Like Bill Russell, Walton is able to hold his position and not attack the ball until a shot is released. . . . "But if you ask me," says Nate Thurmond, "most people put too much emphasis on blocked shots anyway. A guy can block a lot of shots and still be a poor defensive player. Elmore Smith of the Cleveland Cavaliers is always among the league leaders, but Elmore wants to block every shot in sight, and he's constantly drifting away from his own man at the wrong times. A good defensive center will also intimidate a lot of shots and never get any statistical credit when they miss."

Proper communication is far more important to good team defense than blocked shots. A center beholds the entire floor, and he can talk to his teammates and inform them of impending trouble. "It's a great help when your big man talks on defense," says Nate Archibald. "Knowing where the blind-side picks are and knowing when to switch can save some wear and tear on your body." A center should also yell "Ball!" whenever he has a clear shot at a defensive rebound, freeing his teammates from any rebounding responsibilities and sending them flying downcourt on the fast break. To retain his sweep of the field, the defensive center must know exactly where his own man is at all times. "The best way to do this," says Nate Thurmond, "is to keep your hands on your man so you won't have to look at him to know what he's up to. And if you can touch him, you can also try and influence his movements." In the NBA it's this exercise of influence that leads to most of the violence.

The rule book declares that basketball is a noncontact activity, but the NBA game is actually a collision sport that has always been prone to violence. "In the old days," said Joe Lapchick, "playing in the NBA was a test of manhood. The players would immediately put several questions to a newcomer. How much pain and risk was he willing to take? Could he be made to lose his temper and lose control of his game? Would he miss any shots knowing that he was going to get belted afterwards? Could he be worn down physically over the course of the season? The only way to answer these questions was to fight back." The early NBA bigwigs were forever afraid that too many whistles would paralyze the action and deaden the fans' interest. The owners had nightmares of foul-shooting contests conducted inside empty buildings, and they encouraged the refs to call loose ball games. "So long as a rebound was alive," said Lapchick, "there was no such thing as a foul." This shortsighted policy promoted only more and more violence. If a ballplayer got away with six "sternum smashes" out of ten, then he gained still more by trying twenty. . . .

Most of the violence centers on the battle for position near the basket. A choice bit of property with hoop-side frontage means rebounds, playing time, points, and money in a big man's pocket. Guards and forwards can always pursue the ball and then worry about getting good position. But most centers have limited ball-handling skills, and the ball must be brought to them. And no big man can establish himself on the slightest piece of priority acreage without first making a substantial down payment. Not even Wilt Chamberlain. . . .

"FOUL ON WALTER DUKES," barks the public address announcer. "WILT CHAMBERLAIN TO SHOOT TWO."

The big man wears his familiar accoutrements: an orange headband, knee-length socks, and, around his left wrist, a rubber band. Chamberlain bounces the ball slowly and tries to set his feet. But his huge body twitches with discomfort, and his eyes avoid the basket until he suddenly grabs the ball and hastily sights the target. Then he shrugs his shoulders, dips his right hand, and flings the ball at the hoop. . . . The shot is still rising when it slams off the backboard, and even the referee laughs as he retrieves the ball. . . . Chamberlain prepares for his second shot by once again bouncing the ball carefully and staring at the foul line. The big man moves back a step, dips his right hand, and unclenches a helium pop fly that glances off the top half of the backboard and plunges through the hoop.

One look at Chamberlain's foul shooting convinced coaches all over the league of the wisdom of deliberately fouling him in clutch situations. In '59–'60, Chamberlain shot 58 percent from the foul line, yet in practice sessions over 80 percent of his free throws were swisheroos. Chamberlain absorbed a beating every game, and his frustration mounted throughout his rookie season. . . . Then in one memorable ball game against the St. Louis Hawks, Chamberlain tried to evict Clyde Lovellette from the veteran center's favorite watering spot near the basket. Chamberlain employed a variety of threats, scowls, and aggressive leanings, and for a time Lovellette let the bigger man have his way. But the veteran was merely waiting until he had the proper angle, and a few minutes later Lovellette used the Elbow of Experience to shatter four of Chamberlain's front teeth. . . . After the season was over, Chamberlain announced that the NBA was much too violent and that he preferred to retire. The big man eventually decided to resume his livelihood once he realized that all rookies in all professional sports are targeted to "educational violence."

Steve Patterson had a tidy five-year career in the NBA, and he can also attest to the wars that the big men wage against rookies. "I remember my first year with Cleveland in 1971," says Patterson. "Bob Lanier was one of the first guys I faced. I was well aware of Bob's great strength, but I went out there and leaned on him. I mean I hammered him, and I practically hung on him. Well, we were shoving each other pretty good, and I figured I was playing him heads up. . . . Then, all of a sudden, he just wrapped his arm around me and threw me to the ground like I was made of straw. To tell the truth, I still don't know how he did it. I made a complete four-point landing, and I bruised both elbows so badly that I had bone chips for the next few years. But I knew right away that Bob wasn't trying to hurt me. He wasn't even angry, and he was the first one over to give me a hand and help me to my feet. Bob merely gave me a graphic illustration that all right, I could play rough, and I could play strong; but there was a line past which I could not go. The amazing thing is that players will get very physical with you when you're new in the league, but after you battle back, they begin to concede things to you. Once they know you're going to fight them for a certain spot or a certain position, they'll just let you have it. Or when they see that you're going to box out every single time, then they just stop going to the offensive boards against you. Once that line is established, everybody respects it, and the longer you play, the easier it gets."

But rookie centers are by no means the recipients of all the violence in the NBA. Mike Riordan, a 6'4" veteran of nine NBA campaigns, explains the dangers that a small man invites whenever he ventures too close to the basket: "Guys like Elvin Hayes, Wilt, Russell, Thurmond, and Abdul-Jabbar would just block your shot and embarrass you. But there are other big men who don't have the quickness, timing, or jumping ability to do that. So they use other means to discourage you from penetrating and taking liberties under the boards. Guys like Unseld, Reed, Lanier, and Cowens will try and get to your shot, but if they can't reach it, then they'll just knock you on your ass. They'll take the foul, and you'll take a pounding. They want to make you think twice about going to the hoop the next time around. But if you want to stay in the league, you can't let them intimidate you. You simply have to take the punishment. It's better than letting a big man take away part of your game."

A big man must be physical to be effective in the NBA, yet some players go to extraordinary lengths to toughen themselves.

"When Dave Cowens was a rookie," says Don Nelson, currently the coach of the Milwaukee Bucks, "he introduced a game that he called Butting Heads. It was simple. Two guys would bang their heads together until one of them gave up. I could outbutt everybody but Cowens, and he was almost always the champion. After a while the other guys didn't like to play too much, but sometimes we forced them to."

The long history of NBA violence culminated on December 9, 1977, when Kermit Washington slugged Kevin Kunnert to the floor, and then Rudy Tomjanovich ran into a punch that broke his face. The entire country watched the syndicated film clip of the incident in absolute horror. "The hatchet men were rough," said Eddie Gottlieb, the original owner of the Philadelphia Warriors, "but they always gave warning. A guy like Bob Brannum might put a guy away for the night but never for a month." Even the referees were outraged. "In the old days," said Norm Drucker, the NBA's supervisor of officials, "all the fights were face-to-face. There were never any sneak punches like nowadays." The NBA owners were so frightened that during the off-season league meetings they finally approved a third official for '78–'79.

Yet the coaches and players were barely surprised. "Things happen in the heat of a ball game," says Bob Kauffman, a rugged center for seven NBA seasons, "and one thing sometimes leads to another. A big man has to protect himself and make sure that other guys don't try and take advantage of him. Sometimes you have to fight; it's part of the big man's game. You hope it never happens, but you can't afford to back down when it does."

Most coaches agree that violence is inherent in the pro game and will never be eradicated by threat of foul, fine, or suspension. Several coaches suggest that a 30-second shot clock and a 3-point field goal would spread the defense and reduce the body contact. "They better do something quick," one coach warns.

127

"Defense near the basket is hand-to-hand combat, especially away from the ball. Tomjanovich was only moderately maimed, but it's only a matter of time till someone gets killed. As much as I hate to say it, it's true."

The largest, quickest, and strongest centers usually cast the most violent shadows of defensive influence. Yet even the most ferocious big man is reluctant to play gangbusters defense away from the basket. And most NBA centers feel they are doing their teammates a favor whenever they switch. . . . The Sonics are at Chicago and ahead by 1 point in the fourth quarter, when Dennis Johnson runs Bulls' rookie guard Mike Glenn into a solid pick set by 7'1", 245-pound Marvin Webster, and Johnson is suddenly in the clear. . . . Artis Gilmore is the Bulls' center, and he stands a scant 10 feet from Johnson. Gilmore's hands twitch with involuntary defense; but his feet never move, and Johnson cans an easy jump shot. . . .

The NBA's running centers are usually smaller and lighter. They must make up for the mismatches underneath by extending their defensive presence to include the entire court. . . . The Celtics are playing at Indiana, and 6'3" Ricky Sobers and 7'0" James Edwards are trying to entangle 6'3" Jo Jo White and 6'9" Dave Cowens in a pick-and-roll. . . . Sobers succeeds in rubbing White on Edwards's pick, and the Pacers' big man spins to the basket. But Cowens switches eagerly from Edwards to Sobers. And even though they're both 20 feet from the basket, Cowens breathes fire into Sobers's face. Sobers retreats another few steps and then dumps the ball to the weak-side guard. . . . "When Dave Cowens switches on to a guard," says Jo Jo White, "then he stays switched. The little man usually wants no part of a redheaded monster jumping all over the place and waving his arms like crazy. The guard's own big man may be free under the basket, but all the guy wants to do is get rid of the ball and get the hell away from Cowens. It makes for a lot of bad passes and more fast break opportunities for the

Celtics." . . . Besides Cowens, other contemporary running centers have included 6'9" Clifford Ray, 6'9" Alvan Adams, 6'8" Bob Kauffman, 6'8" Phil Jackson, 6'8" John Hummer, 6'8" Spencer Haywood, 6'8" Lonnie Shelton, and 6'7" Lloyd Neal.

If there's room in the NBA for an occasional small center, there's always a spot for an awkward 7-footer—Vic Bartolome, Bob Christian, Greg Fillmore, Swede Halbrook, Len Kosmalski, Ebberle Neil, Dave Newmark, Rich Niemann, Tom Payne, Ralph Siewert, and Craig Spitzer. "Clumsy centers" can stumble and flop around in the pivot and still contribute something positive—like keeping the ball alive on the offensive boards and creating confusion.

A quality big man is the most precious commodity in the NBA. There are only six active centers who have started on championship ball clubs—Kareem Abdul-Jabbar, Clifford Ray, Dave Cowens, Bill Walton, and either Wes Unseld or Elvin Hayes.

The big man is always the Prime Mover of his ball club. If he must play in the pivot with his back to the basket, then his team is forced into deliberate offense, and the roster must be top-heavy with good outside shooters. If a center can play the high post and face the basket, then the middle is open to penetration, and his team can utilize a quicker, more diversified offense. Ball clubs powered by offensive-minded centers occasionally turn into winners. But a team built around a talented center with an appetite for defense will always prosper. . . .

Because everybody sacrifices when the Big Man sacrifices.

CENTERS

	PASSING	SPEED	CREATING OWN SHOT	SPOT SHOOTING	SHOT SELECTION	SCORING	EFFECTIVENESS W/O BALL	DEFENSIVE POSITION	DEFENSIVE ANTICIPATION	STRENGTH	OFFENSIVE REBOUNDING	DEFENSIVE REBOUNDING	CONSISTENCY	VERSATILITY	DURABILITY	TOTAL
Bill Russell	4	3	2	2	4	3	4	4	4	4	4	4	4	4	4	54
Bill Walton	4	3	3	4	4	3	4	4	4	3	3	4	4	4	2	53
Wilt Chamberlain	4	1	4	1	3	4	4	4	4	4	4	4	4	4	4	53
George Mikan	4	1	4	3	4	4	3	4	2	4	4	4	4	3	4	52
Dave Cowens	3	3	2	3	4	3	4	4	4	4	3	4	4	3	3	51
Nate Thurmond	3	2	3	2	3	3	3	4	4	4	4	4	4	3	4	50
Wes Unseld	4	1	1	3	4	2	4	4	3	4	4	4	4	3	4	49
Kareem Abdul-Jabbar	3	2	4	3	4	4	2	3	4	4	2	4	4	2	3	48
Artis Gilmore	2	1	4	2	3	4	3	4	3	4	4	4	3	2	4	47
Bob McAdoo	1	4	4	4	3	4	2	2	3	2	3	4	3	4	4	47
Willis Reed	2	1	4	3	4	4	3	4	3	4	2	3	4	3	3	47
Alvan Adams	4	4	2	4	4	3	3	3	3	2	3	3	3	3	2	46
Bob Lanier	2	2	4	4	4	4	2	3	2	4	3	3	3	3	3	46
Dan Issel	2	2	2	4	4	4	4	3	2	3	2	2	4	4	4	46
Billy Paultz	3	1	3	4	4	3	3	3	3	4	2	2	3	3	4	45
Swen Nater	2	1	3	3	3	4	4	2	4	3	4	3	3	2	4	45
Clifford Ray	2	3	2	1	4	2	4	3	4	4	3	3	3	2	4	44
Jim Chones	2	4	4	4	3	3	2	3	2	3	2	3	2	3	4	44
Sam Lacey	4	3	2	2	3	2	3	3	3	3	2	4	2	2	4	42
Marvin Webster	1	3	3	3	3	2	2	2	3	4	4	4	2	2	3	41
Moses Malone	1	4	3	2	3	3	2	2	2	3	4	4	2	2	4	41

LEGEND
4 = outstanding   3 = good   2 = average   1 = poor

12

THE OBSOLESCENCE
OF TRADITION

The mortgage on New York City is long overdue. Criminals and
junkies roam the streets. The slums are rubble. The air is
poisoned. The beaches are sludged. And the Knicks are lousy.
Millions of New Yorkers live in terror, and millions are stung
with despair. They seek to survive by fantasizing, meditating,
boozing, doping, worrying, protesting, scheming, felonizing,
partying, and Jonesing through their workaday lives. . . . The
task is always easier for the city's basketball fans, especially
those whose souls are still warmed by the championship after-
glow of 1970 and 1973. Knick Freaks cope by throwing
surreptitious behind-the-back passes with empty beer cans, by
shooting secret game winners with crumpled garbage. For
them, the Knick glories have long since condensed into proof of
a dream come true. . . . When every Knick game was a
psychodrama. When the cry of "Dee-fense!" was a moral
imperative hurled at the players and at God. Back when every
Knick victory brought a rush of righteousness. "Knick fans are
the greatest," Bill Bradley used to say. "They help us win ball
games." And the Knick Freaks thought their basketball nirvana
would last forever. But then Dave DeBusschere retired in his

prime, Willis Reed's legs gave out, and Jerry Lucas grew old in a hurry. The seasons always toll quickly in New York, and none of the Knicks' draft picks—Tom Riker, Mel Davis, Jesse Dark, or Eugene Short—could recapture the rapture.

By '74–'75 the Knicks were 20 games out of first place, and their fans were growing restless. Then, in 1975, Spencer Haywood was secured from the Seattle SuperSonics in exchange for Eugene Short and cash. Haywood blew into town sporting a lifetime NBA average of 24.9 ppg. "I am the reincarnation of Dave DeBusschere," said Haywood. "I am the restorer of the dynasty." And the desperate Knick Freaks eagerly hailed him as their savior.

Spencer Haywood first bolted into basketball prominence in 1968, when he catapulted the United States Olympic hoopsters to a gold medal in Mexico City. Haywood was nineteen, a junior college graduate, rapier-quick, sharpshooting, and thriving under coach Hank Iba's discipline. Haywood's scintillating performance in the Olympics earned him a scholarship to the University of Detroit. The Titans were coached by Bob Calihan, a veteran of twenty-one seasons at UD. Haywood was remarkably resistant to Calihan's coaching, but he collected impressive statistics on a mediocre team. Then, in the summer of 1969, Haywood became professional basketball's first "hardship" draftee when he signed a handsome contract with the Denver Rockets of the ABA. Haywood was blissfully ignorant of basketball fundamentals, and he had no conception of how to run a play. But the competition was meager, and Haywood's wild and woolly game was the scourge of the league. Haywood led the ABA in scoring and rebounding, and he was honored as Rookie of the Year, First Team All-Star, and Most Valuable Player. With no horizons left to conquer, Haywood cited the Rockets for several contract violations and jumped to the Seattle SuperSonics. Haywood's game was still limited, but his turnaround jumper going right to the base line proved to be as effective in the NBA as it was in the ABA. "Spencer was a great basketball player," says a former Seattle teammate, "but he was never in one place long enough to learn how to play the game. Everything came so easy for him, and he had trouble dealing with authority. To make matters worse, Haywood had four coaches during his first three seasons in Seattle. Then Bill Russell became the Sonics' coach in 1973, and Russ tried to take over everybody's lives. Spencer just couldn't deal with Russell at all, and he was thrilled to be sent to New York." But Haywood was too insecure to be comfortable with the unselfish, disciplined game preached by Red Holzman. Nor did Haywood ever master the intricacies of Holzman's offense, and the Knicks continued to decline.

The Knicks' next store-bought Messiah was 6'11" Bob McAdoo, the NBA's leading point maker from 1974 to 1976. Knick Freaks were easily convinced that Haywood and McAdoo would be irresistible together; but both players were scoring forwards who needed the ball to be useful, and their skills overlapped. In addition, there was too much defensive pressure placed on the third member of the Knicks' front line (variously Jim McMillian, Tom McMillen, Lonnie Shelton, and Phil Jackson), and the team lost its balance whenever Haywood and McAdoo shared the floor.

McAdoo was a much more dynamic scorer than Haywood, so the Knicks' offense was pointed at him. For public consumption, Haywood espoused satisfaction and togetherness, but it was obvious that McAdoo and he were incompatible. . . . The Knicks' bus is heading back to New York after a humiliating loss in Philadelphia. Haywood is sitting directly in front of McAdoo, and he clips forty-five minutes of jazz into his portable tape machine. McAdoo is gobbling a tuna fish sandwich and being interviewed by sportswriter Mark Ribowsky. "When Spencer puts that stuff on," says McAdoo, "I tune out. Jazz makes me nervous." Haywood immediately turns around and faces McAdoo. "This is *Herbie Hancock,* man," says Haywood. "This is *art*. Not like that shit you listen to." McAdoo crinkles his nose with distaste and then slips a Parliament-Funkadelic tape into his own machine. McAdoo dons a pair of headphones, switches off the overhead light, and terminates the interview. . . .

Willis Reed took over for Red Holzman in 1977, but the team remained plagued with petty jealousies, forced shots, and hesitancy in the clutch. A former Knick player suggested that the team had the IQ of an orangutan, the weekly NBA stats proved that the Knicks also had the most embarrassing defense in the league. The Knick Freaks were shocked and utterly bewildered. New Yorkers can find something to love in black-outs, subway strikes, and even bumbling ball clubs like the early Mets. But the new Knicks were so dramatically stupid and so obviously a lie. And the loving Jonesness of the championship years slowly turned to arrogance and cynicism.

The '77–'78 edition of the New York Knicks is warming up at the Sixth Avenue end of Madison Square Garden. Their opponents are the Seattle SuperSonics, and the arena is five thousand customers shy of capacity. The stands are spotted with teenagers in scruffy sneakers, with doctors, lawyers, teachers, businessmen, and professional wise guys. But movie stars no longer flock to see the Knicks, and most of the fans are new to the game—"Daddy, which one is Bob McAdoo?"

Bill Bradley is a senator, Dave DeBusschere is a stockbroker, Clyde is a Cavalier, and nobody's seen Dick Barnett in years. But as the Knicks and Sonics lope through their pregame paces, there are several ghosts on hand: There's Willis Reed, now the coach, and Phil Jackson, now a bench warmer. The Pearl still starts at guard; but he's thirty-four years old, and his knees are filling with sand.

The fans are wary as the players are introduced. Their most fervent cheers belong to Monroe, and they listlessly hoot at the Sonics.

"Ladies and gentlemen," booms John Condon, the public

address announcer. "Jim McMillian of the Knickerbockers will not be playing tonight because of an illness."

The news is unfortunate but not sinister, yet the fans are instantly charged with hostility, and by the thousands, they jump to their feet and scream abuse at the absent McMillian. Several Knick players turn and trade curses with the nearby fans.

Bob McAdoo is smoking as the game gets under way and the locals are staked to an early 13-point lead. But the fans remain suspicious. They expect the Knicks to collapse. They expect to get mugged on the way home. A hopeful chorus of "Dee-fense!" is stifled when Dennis Johnson drives through three Knicks and scores a lay-up. McAdoo's shots stop falling, and the Knicks close the first half with a precarious 6-point lead.

The home team quickly disintegrates after the intermission. Their defense becomes a rumor, and they have trouble completing a pass. The fans begin to jeer, and the Sonics stretch to a 19-point lead early in the last period. The Knicks on the bench are bristling with anger as the catcalls get obscene.

Then, with 10 minutes to go, Lonnie Shelton, Toby Knight, and Ray Williams engineer an improbable Knick flurry that threatens to make the score competitive. But the fans refuse to assume the risk of total involvement until the Sonics' lead is trimmed to 6. The Knicks sustain their rally and surge at the buzzer to win, 112–110. The fans are jubilant and flushed with celebration. But most of them make speedy exits so they can journey to their parking lots, subways, cabs, buses, and commuter trains encased in the dubious safety of a crowd.

In the Knick locker room the miraculous victory has not calmed the players, and they are anxious to snipe at the fans. "The New York fans are vicious," says one player. "I always play better on the road."

"They're front-runners," chimes another.

"The fans don't know any better," says Earl Monroe. "Their

lack of insight is created and perpetuated by the economic realities of the game. All season long, management tells everybody that the players have got to sacrifice to win. But when it comes to contract negotiations, all management wants to discuss is the stat sheet. 'You didn't do such-and-such,' they say. 'Here it is right here.' If management thinks so little of a player's ability to play a role, then the fans don't have a chance."

"The Garden fans support our stars," says Phil Jackson, "the guys who look flashy on the court. But they have no appreciation for the other guys who are out there working hard every night and doing the little things that are just as important. I think the players' egos and the absence of public and financial recognition are the biggest reasons why there are so few successful role players in the NBA."

It's always a constant struggle for an NBA coach to set and maintain roles for his players. Some coaches try charisma, some use con, some dispense praise, others threats. . . . When Tom Heinsohn first became coach of the Celtics, he was a beefy 245 pounds, yet he was still in good enough condition to scrimmage occasionally with the team. "We had one rookie who wanted to be a shooting forward," reports one Celtic veteran. "The only problem was that Heinsohn and Auerbach had him pegged as a power forward. The kid would nod his head and agree with everything he was told. Then he'd go right on shooting from the outside and tiptoeing around the boards. So the Hawk used to match himself against the rookie in practice. The kid was quick and strong; but Heinsohn had all that NBA experience, and he beat the living shit out of the rookie. Every day. But the treatment didn't work. The rookie had a no-cut, and he wouldn't change his game. . . ."

There remains only one dependable way to make a professional basketball player gladly accept a role—the way of tradition.

J. Howard McHugh is a sprightly sexagenarian who handles public relations for the Boston Celtics. His eyes are blue and friendly, his face is folded with peaceable wrinkles, and his handshake is as warming as his smile. Howie McHugh even likes Sidney Wicks. "Sidney's a nice fellow," says Howie, "and I think he works harder than most people realize. The only complaint I have about Sidney is that he has bad hands. . . . Cheez! He's got those clang hands. . . !"

Howie McHugh has a proper Bostonian mania for the Bruins, the Red Sox, and, reluctantly, the Patriots. "I was originally a hockey player," Howie confesses. "I played for the old Boston Olympians in the late thirties. Then for a while I was the spare goalie for the Bruins. But that isn't as impressive as it sounds. I was around just so the Bruins could skate from end-to-end in practice. Then I got hurt, and I started doing public relations work for Walter Brown, who owned the Bruins and the Boston Garden. I was in the navy during the war, and when I got out, basketball was bigger in Boston than hockey. So I switched over when Brown started the Celtics. I've been here since the beginning. Since even before Auerbach."

Howie McHugh had already been typing press releases for four years when Auerbach arrived in Boston in the summer of 1950. Walter Brown was a businessman, so he gave Auerbach free reign and full support in running the ball club. Auerbach quickly instituted a "system" that was based on fast breaks, respect, moving without the ball, hustle, boxing out, courage, and defense and was implemented through role playing.

Over the years the Celtics' indoctrination procedure also became systematic. Whenever a newcomer joined the team, the coach would take him aside and break the Celtics' game plan into easily digestible components. The new man was shown exactly where the shots were and what all the other players' responsibilities were. Every player learned every play from every position. Then, after a while, the coach would ask the new player where he felt most comfortable. Which role did he think he could play best. Sometimes the choice was obvious: Sam Jones's spectacular shooting would have been foolishly wasted had he become a defensive guard. Paul Silas could never have been anything but a power forward. But sometimes the situation dictated the role a ballplayer had to assume. When Dave Cowens was drafted by the Celtics in 1970, he was ideally equipped to become the finest power forward in the history of Western civilization. But the team's most pressing need was for a center. Over the summer, Auerbach sent Cowens to Harlem to play center for the "Bronx Celtics" in the Rucker League. Then Bill Russell was brought into training camp to test, tutor, and pronounce Cowens fit for the job. Most Celtic rookies looked forward to long apprenticeships on the bench—it was nine years before John Havlicek was allowed to start. But the Celtics' exigency was so urgent in '70–'71 that Cowens averaged almost thirty-eight minutes a game as a rookie.

"The Celtics always had veteran players around to help break in the new men," Howie McHugh remembers. "Cousy and Sharman taught Havlicek and the Jones boys. Then Sam, K.C., and Hondo showed Jo Jo White the ropes. Everybody always helped everybody else. The ballplayers knew they were going to win, and the sportswriters called it Celtic Pride. But you can't have tradition without stability and continuity. So Cousy was a Celtic for thirteen years, Sam Jones for twelve, K.C. for nine, Russell for thirteen, Sanders for twelve, Heinsohn for nine, White for ten, and Havlicek forever. Continuity also means consistency, and consistency is the secret of winning in the NBA.

Then Howie McHugh leans back from his desk and slowly stirs a plastic cup of coffee. And for a moment, his blue eyes seem to twinkle with a greenish leprechaun glow. "I guess you could call that tradition," he says with a chuckle. "I dunno. Havlicek used to say all that tradition stuff was the invention of the media."

But in the summer of 1978 the respective owners of the Buffalo Braves and the Boston Celtics traded franchises and also completed a massive exchange of players. . . . Irving Levin is a lawyer and Hollywood film mogul who controlled the Celtics for four years without ever feeling completely at ease in Boston. Levin moved his new team to San Diego, and he expressed hearty satisfaction at securing veterans Kermit Washington, Kevin Kunnert, and Sidney Wicks, along with rookie Freeman Williams from Boston in exchange for Nate Archibald, Marvin ("The Baddest News") Barnes, and Billy Knight. "Everybody back east thinks I raped Boston and stole their best players," said Levin. "And I think I did, too."

The Celtics' new boss is John Y. Brown, a fried-chicken magnate who owned the Braves for one year and the ABA Kentucky Colonels for six years. John Y. is reputed to be a "polished charmer," who insists that the most offensive basketball team is invariably the best. John Y. didn't deem it necessary to consult the Celtics' coaching staff (Tom Sanders and K.C. Jones) about the wholesale player moves. Nor did John Y. bother to inform Red Auerbach. "After a total of seven years in professional basketball," said John Y., "I think I know the game. Heck, if I'd studied medicine that long, I'd be a doctor."

When the feathers finally settled, the Buffalo Braves became the San Diego Clippers, while the Celtics retained their coaches, players Curtis Rowe, Jo Jo White, and Dave Cowens, their name, their logos, Red Auerbach, and Howie McHugh. But the Celtic fans were distraught at the prospect of having to root for the infamous Marvin Barnes. "There is a general suspicion," wrote Ernie Roberts of the *Boston Evening Globe,* "that we are getting the NBA version of Reggie Jackson and George Steinbrenner, that Celtic Pride will become Yankee Turbulence." But John Y. moved quickly to soothe the populace.

After a lengthy chat with Barnes, John Y. summoned a press conference. "My career in the NBA has been a big disappointment so far," admitted Barnes. "I've been too fat-cattish. I have three years and nine hundred and fifty thousand dollars left on my original seven-year contract, but I don't want a no-cut anymore. If I don't produce for the Celtics, then I want them to be able to drop me from the team. I want that kind of pressure working on me. I'm determined to be a productive member of the team and to help restore Celtic Pride. This is something I have to do as a man."

John Y. also added that Levin's assessment of the massive trade was inaccurate. "Levin is out of his tree," said John Y. "We're getting three proven players for three who have yet to distinguish themselves in the NBA. And we've also gotten rid of a player, Sidney Wicks, who was not wanted by any other team in the league." John Y. dismissed Kermit Washington as "a limited player, a role player."

While all this was happening, Red Auerbach strolled around the room, smiling through his cigar and saying, "I have good vibes, very good vibes about this Celtic team." The Boston sportswriters took one collective gulp and hailed the reconstruction of the Celtic tradition.

Meanwhile, Howie McHugh sat at a corner table, neatly draining another cup of coffee. "I dunno," said Howie. "Now we've got a bunch of guys who can score like hell. We'll just have to wait and see if they can do anything else. But I will admit we have a lot more talent now than we ended up with last year. And I also know that both Jo Jo and Dave are anxious to play. But cheez. . . . I sure hated to see Kermit Washington go. As far as I'm concerned, he's paid his dues in full, and he's already one of the best power forwards in the league. I'm also glad that Auerbach decided to turn down an offer from the Knicks and stay in Boston. Not everybody likes Red, but he does make a difference."

Howie McHugh is an honest man in a tricky business. His continuing presence is somehow a testimonial to the basic health and wholesomeness of the entire NBA. "Satch Sanders looks like he has the makings of a great coach," says Howie. "Satch snarls and yells, and all the ballplayers seem to understand him. I dunno. I guess things started to change about five years ago. Most of the old-time players would have played for nothing. Cheez. . . . Maybe understanding is the latest thing. I dunno. But I don't think understanding can be any good without continuity and without loyalty. Not in the NBA. Not anywhere."

After each NBA season the league's rosters are shaken like dice. . . . The liberties of free agency send Rick Barry to Houston, Mike Glenn to New York, Gus Williams to Seattle, Alex English and Kevin Stacom to Indiana, E. C. Coleman to Golden State, Gail Goodrich to New Orleans, and the likes of Earl Monroe, David Thompson, and Marvin Webster shopping around the league. For every free agent who changes ball clubs, another player is also shipped out as "compensation." (The lone exception being Jamaal Wilkes, who moved from Golden State to Los Angeles in 1976. NBA commissioner Larry O'Brien decreed that the Warriors' compensation would be $200,000. "That's just great," said Al Attles, coach and general manager of the Warriors. "Next year I'll start four ballplayers and a pile of money.")

The adjudicated illegality of the reserve clause has been a boon of riches and freedom to many professional athletes. But too much freedom can also lead to chains. . . . Len ("Truck") Robinson came out of Tennessee State in 1974 as the second-round draft choice of the Washington Bullets, and he was signed to a three-year no-cut pact. The 6'7", 230-pound Robinson played two and a half erratic seasons behind Elvin Hayes and Wes Unseld before he was traded to Atlanta in January 1977. Hubie Brown provided Robinson with a full load of playing time, and Truck suddenly began to rumble the backboards and accelerate his scoring. But four months later Robinson became a free agent and accepted a monstrous contract to play for the New Orleans Jazz. At Robinson's insistence, New Orleans also added a clause declaring that Truck could not be traded without unilateral consent. In '77–'78

Robinson averaged 15.7 rebounds a game for the Jazz, thereby becoming the first forward to lead the NBA in rebounding since Harry Gallatin in '53–'54. Robinson also tickled the twines for 22.7 ppg and was named to the postseason All-Star team. But Robinson was very unhappy at New Orleans. "There are two sets of rules on the Jazz," he said. "One for Pete Maravich and one for everyone else. I want to be traded." But the New Orleans ownership refused to accommodate Robinson's demand. They pointed to the no-trade clause in Robinson's contract as binding on both the team and the player.

No championship team has repeated since the Celtics won in 1968 and 1969, and each new NBA season has become an exercise in existentialism. "It's impossible to build a solid ball club these days," says one disgruntled NBA coach, "and the overall quality of play is definitely on the wane. The Washington Bullets, for example, had to be the worst championship team in years. Wes Unseld was the only guy willing to sacrifice, and everybody else took turns going one-on-one. It's nuts. During the final series against Seattle, both Bobby Dandridge and Elvin Hayes said that Unseld should be benched because he wasn't scoring enough. . . . Sure, the Bullets did win the championship. But that's only because *somebody's* got to win."

It's a new age in the NBA. Ballplayers' loyalties are strictly pragmatic, and they willfully disregard the necessity of role playing. As a result, NBA action threatens to become increasingly spectacular, but shallow and flabby as well. . . . On the last day of the '77–'78 regular season David Thompson and George Gervin were contending for the league's scoring title. The Nuggets finished on a Sunday afternoon in Detroit— Thompson played forty-three minutes and scored 73 points on 28–38 from the field and 17–20 from the foul line. The Spurs' ball game was played later that evening in New Orleans, and Gervin knew that he needed 58 points to overtake Thompson. In just thirty-three minutes of play, Gervin amassed 49 shots from the floor, 20 free throws, and 1 assist. Gervin's final total of 63 points earned him the scoring crown by .07 ppg. Basketball fans all over the country were lit up by the outrageous shoot-out. But few of them noticed that both the Nuggets and the Spurs lost their ball games. . . .

Tradition has been annihilated, and the accountants are the new high priests.

13
THE PERFECT PLAYER

Evaluating NBA talent is more complicated than just determining how well a certain player fits a certain role. Like any good game, basketball is beautiful and meaningful because it reveals the inner nature of the players. Since a player's performance can be only a manifestation of his reason for playing, the basic measure of his real effectiveness is his motivation.

Some players play to the fans, some for the numbers, and some to fuel their egos. But the good ones play for each other, and the great ones seek perfection. "I sometimes get mad during a ball game because of some silly mistake I've made," says Dave Cowens. "It might look like I'm mad at someone else, but I'm really upset with myself. My ambition is to play a perfect ball game, both offensively and defensively. Not too many people will know if it ever happens. But I will."

Motivation always reduces to personal dignity and self-esteem. . . . When Connie Hawkins was with the Phoenix Suns, his casual attitude toward ball games was a continuing mystery to coach Jerry Colangelo. On one particular evening Hawkins arrived at the arena and complained to Colangelo of having a fever. The Suns' physician was immediately summoned to examine Hawkins and take his temperature.

"It's 99.2," said the doctor.

"I told you I was sick," said Hawkins. "I'm not playing."

"Connie!" said the exasperated Colangelo. "Don't you have any pride?"

"No," said Hawkins.

Concentration is a living awareness of the changing game situation, a steady focus on the eternal moment. Concentration is pride in action. Concentration is self-generating, but even the most veteran players believe they can play carelessly and then tighten their grasp of the game when they must. "You can't turn it on and off," says Jack Marin. "No matter how good you are. What happens when you try is that you fall behind early and then you have to gamble and play catch-up for the rest of the game. You've got to be totally involved all the time. Even when you're on the bench."

The imagined security of long-term no-cut contracts can easily undermine a ballplayer's attention to the game at hand. So can the ladies, and every year dozens of players contend for the NBA's All-Lobby Team. "Anywhere on the road," says an NBA trouper, "all you have to do is scout the lobby to find some pussy." The widespread use of drugs in the NBA constitutes another major distraction: The average NBA ballplayer is twenty-five years old, and he shares the same interest in "getting high" as do millions of his contemporaries. Most ball players are wise enough to save their cocaine and marijuana until the game is over. But once in a while a player in severe emotional distress will get stoned for a game. There have also been a number of players who were blackballed from the league because of cocaine "addiction." But NBA players are usually very careful about their "party drugs."

At least half of the players in the league regularly indulge in cocaine and/or marijuana, but nobody uses amphetamines. "I think the biggest reason why NBA players use so few pills," says Stan Love, "is that we play too much. Let's say the season starts out with a game every other night, and each time you take a pill to get up. By midseason the schedule starts getting crowded, and you often play four games in five nights. It won't be long before you start developing a tolerance, and to get the right effect, you'll have to take two or three a night. By the time you get to the eighty-second game you'll be fried. It's not like football, where the players only need speed twenty times a year and have a week off between games to let the effects wear off. Another reason why basketball players avoid pills is that touch is everything in basketball and Dexedrine ruins touch. If you're too wired up, you can run into guys and foul them without even knowing what you're doing."

The NBA is also loaded with drugs that are far more destructive than speed, coke, or pot. Including exhibition games and play-offs, the average team plays about 100 ball games a season. In '77–'78, NBA training camps were officially convened on September 21, and the championship wasn't decided until June 7. The long season, the continuous traveling, and the ferocious body contact mean that by the All-Star break every player in the league is nursing a bothersome injury. In order to keep them playing, the ballplayers are often given pain-killing drugs (such as Xylocaine) and anti-inflammatories (such as Butazolidin). Coaches and team physicians make these drugs readily available without warning the players of the dangers involved. The side effects of the drugs—weakened muscles, eye damage, and severe depression—frequently compound the players' injuries. Superstars like Bill Walton can safely protest drug abuse—Walton reported that one Portland teammate was shot so full of pain-killers that he knew he broke his shinbone only because he heard the bone snap. But a marginal player either performs when he's hurt or loses his job. Rod Derline, a journeyman guard for the Seattle SuperSonics, was encouraged to play on an injured leg and as a consequence may now be crippled for life.

In the NBA, "life" translates into 2.7 years, the length of the average playing career. Some careers are recorded on flash paper—Forest Able, George Brown, Blaine Denning, Jarrett Durham, Dick Eichhorst, Normie Glick, Dave Gunther, Nat Hickey, Pete Lalich, Jack McCloskey, Carl McNulty, Paul Nolen, Ray Radziszewski, Dave Scholz, Tom Smith, Jim Spruill, Bill Stricker, Roger Strickland, and Stan Washington each lasted only one ball game. . . . A minute or two, maybe a shot, perhaps even a point—Denning scored 5 and McCloskey 6 inside the bubble of a dream. . . . At the other extreme are John Havlicek (1,270 regular season games in sixteen years), Hal Greer (1,122 in fifteen), Paul Silas (1,090 in fourteen), Lenny Wilkens (1,077 in fifteen), Dolph Schayes (1,059 in sixteen), and Johnny Green (1,057 in fourteen).

Superior talent is the only sure way to longevity, but a supplementary blessing must also include a natural resistance to injury. All professional athletes live on the edge of a sudden injury, and the list of shattered NBA careers is top-heavy with pain—Mel Hutchins (knee), Luke Jackson (knee), Ernie Vandeweghe (knee), Willis Reed (knee), Jerry Sloan (knee), Billy Cunningham (knee), Eddie Miles (Achilles' tendon), Kenny Sears (broken jaw). A few players make complete recoveries from grievous injuries—Dick Barnett's career survived a snapped Achilles' tendon, and Phil Jackson played for nine years after a spinal fusion. But the vast majority never fully heal.

Joe Caldwell was as quick as a wish before he went down with a torn knee while playing for the Carolina Cougars in 1971. The damage was actually less severe than the doctors anticipated, and the surgery was considered successful. Caldwell undertook his rehabilitation with diligence, and he was returned to the active list within six months. But Caldwell couldn't forget the agony and the trauma, nor was he totally convinced of his own well-being. The ecstasy of his talent was shrouded with fear, and his game became passive and self-protective. Caldwell lingered with diminishing skills until the Carolina franchise folded in 1975. Caldwell's long-term no-cut paychecks were suddenly terminated, and he sued the ownership and the league for breach of contract. The resolution of the lawsuit consumed nearly five years and most of Caldwell's savings. Caldwell eventually won the case; but he is a bitter man, and his knee still aches whenever the weather changes. . . .

There are several guidelines to good NBA health—a proper diet, adequate rest, and staying in shape during the off-season. Kinesiological studies also indicate that athletes with loose and flexible bodies suffer fewer and milder injuries. But a ballplayer falls a thousand times a season, he gets overpowered, he gets blindsided, he gets submarined, he dives, he slips, and he trips. "Everybody gets banged around," says Dave Cowens. "I've always found that the best way to avoid serious injuries is to play aggressively and not even think of the possibility of getting hurt."

Only ballplayers with aces in talent, motivation, concentration, and durability can be consistent winners in the NBA. Yet there are times in every ball game when consistency is insufficient. The mark of a truly great player—like George Mikan, Ernie Vandeweghe, Bob Pettit, Bob Cousy, Sam Jones, John Havlicek, Bill Russell, Dave Cowens, Oscar Robertson, Jerry West, Walt Frazier, Dave DeBusschere—is his ability to peak in the clutch.

Most NBA players are eager to prove their capabilities in pressure situations. A few are not. . . . Luke Jackson was a 6'9", 240-pounder out of Pan American College who was a starting forward for the Philadelphia 76ers in '65–'66, his second year in the league. Jackson was a quick power forward with a streaky jump shot and the strength of a center. Chet Walker, Hal Greer, Billy Cunningham, and Wilt Chamberlain accounted for nearly 70 percent of the team's attempted field goals, and Jackson averaged only 7.7 shots and 8.2 points in twenty-five minutes a game. Jackson also played rugged defense and was the team's second leading rebounder behind Chamberlain.

Philadelphia was still a year away from the championship, but they were awesome during the '65–'66 regular season. The 76ers had the best record in the league, and they beat out the "Auerrussellbach" Celtics for first place in the Eastern Division.

The Celtics revived quickly once the play-offs began, and they faced Philadelphia in the semifinal round. Chamberlain returned from an injury to average 28 points and 30 rebounds a game against Russell. Greer, Walker, and Cunningham were stymied by the Celtic defense. Luke Jackson was consistently embarrassed by veterans Tom Sanders and Don Nelson, and the Celtics won the series in only 5 games.

Ballplayers have traditionally blamed their teammates, the officials, their coach, and the media for their own shaky performances. One player dismissed a seasonful of disasters in the clutch as "a long slump." But after the Celtic series, Luke Jackson assumed the full onus of Philadelphia's collapse. "It was all my fault," said the twenty-four-year-old Jackson. "I choked in the clutch."

The word is usually avoided in the media, but *choke* is the worst curse that the grapevine can hang around a ballplayer's career. A player will always have difficulty whenever he becomes too self-conscious and too afraid of failure, whenever he watches himself playing the game instead of allowing the action to absorb his ego. Then every missed shot, turnover, or defensive mishap increases his frustration. He attempts to win the ball game all by himself. But in the end, he overruns the natural boundaries of his own basketball instincts, and he creates tension, confusion, and defeat.

The symptoms are easily discerned: irrelevant hustle on defense; hesitation on offense; perhaps a jump shot that can't avoid the front rim. Yet there are mitigating circumstances which can produce the same unfortunate results. . . . The underdog Knicks are battling the Denver Nuggets in Madison Square Garden, and only a transcendent effort by David Thompson has kept the visitors ahead. With less than a minute to play, the Knicks have the ball and a 1-point deficit. Bob McAdoo is the Knicks' leading scorer so far, with 35 points in forty-six grueling minutes, so New York runs a play that deposits McAdoo in the pivot, gives him the ball, and clears out a side.

McAdoo is defended by Bobby Jones, who leans hard against the bigger man's right shoulder and snipes at the ball. McAdoo is off-balance as he swivels toward the base line to protect the ball from Jones. . . . McAdoo holds the ball for several moments, intent more on passing than dribbling or shooting. . . . Then the Knick bench starts screaming the time, so McAdoo executes two belly-high dribbles to his left on his belated way to find a shot. But Jones easily deflects the ball, and it bounces to Thompson, who races downcourt and jams a lid on the game. . . . "It's ridiculous to say that Bob McAdoo chokes," says George McGinnis. "Hell, I can remember a play-off series in 1976, when he was with Buffalo and I was with Philadelphia. Mac hit two foul shots with one second left to send a ball game into overtime. Then he shot us out of our own building to win the series."

When McAdoo played with Buffalo, all the other players bent their games to suit him, and he was decisive in the clutch. Then McAdoo came to New York, where most of the players were so into themselves that they scarcely spoke to each other. To compound his miseries, the slender McAdoo was forced to play center and suffer a fearful pounding night after night. If McAdoo wasn't strong enough to play the middle, he also had a distressing tendency to wait for the referees to protect him. But NBA officials always dangle their whistles in the closing minutes of a tight ball game, and most players respond by getting extra physical. When he was miscast as a center on a team that didn't dote on him, Bob McAdoo usually dried up and got knocked over in clutch situations.

In all professional sports, no situation is more poignant with significance than the play-offs. . . . "The regular season is just a warm-up for a solid veteran ball club," says one NBA player. "The old Celtic teams, the Knicks, and the Lakers in the early seventies . . . they would all use the regular season to jockey for play-off position, to try to psych out potential play-off rivals, and to work on personnel combinations. A veteran player wants to build up to the play-offs, and a lot of guys never get their legs in good shape until the season is half over. When Bill Russell was around, the Celtics wouldn't begin tying up their loose ends until their annual January road trip. Look at all those years when the Celtics didn't finish first in the regular season but went on to win the championship. Man, everybody knew that Russell never slept more than four hours a night until the play-offs began. But then he would sleep like a monk and go out and play like the next championship would be his first."

In the NBA, play-offs are so contentious that a stellar performance in a single ball game can open up a player's entire career. . . . In '68–'69, Mike Riordan averaged a meager 2.3 ppg for the Knicks and was used primarily to commit strategic fouls. But when Walt Frazier pulled a groin muscle, Riordan was asked to start the sixth game of the Eastern Division finals. The Knicks were overmatched against the title-bound Celtics. But Riordan drove the middle, challenged Russell, and tallied 21 points to pace the Knicks to a courageous 106–105 defeat. The ball game terminated the Knicks' season, but Riordan had unexpectedly demonstrated his excellence. Riordan was suddenly a valuable commodity, and in '69–'70, he became the Knicks' third guard behind Frazier and Dick Barnett. New York had originally signed Riordan for carfare, but in 1971 they were able to package him with Dave Stallworth and complete a trade for the priceless Pearl. Riordan went on to become an outstanding small forward with the Baltimore-Capital-Washington Bullets.

Mike Riordan can also testify to the instant advantages of being left-handed. "In the heat of the moment," says Riordan, "a lot of players sometimes forget who they are guarding. Their unconscious tendency is to overplay everybody to their right.

Being a lefty also means that a right-handed shooter is releasing his shot into my quickest and strongest side." But many of the touchstones of greatness yield only to extensive scouting of games and practice sessions and a lengthy personal interview.

Yet there is a shortcut, a single infallible way to locate and anticipate a superior professional basketball player. . . . When Jerry Lucas and John Havlicek played for Ohio State, Lucas was universally considered the better pro prospect. As a collegian Lucas was a fantastic pivot man who played with grace and intelligence. Havlicek was the team's second banana, and he played the best part of his game without the ball. But Lucas was only 6'8", and his knees were bad, so he had to learn how to play away from the basket to survive in the pros. . . . The true thoroughbred—like Havlicek, Robertson, West, Russell, or Frazier—is the one who can play the same role in the NBA as he did in college.

14

THE PERFECT GAME

The Baltimore Orioles are taking batting practice prior to a baseball game at Yankee Stadium. The second-stringers, bat-boys, coaches, and pitchers do the fielding, while each batter in the Orioles' starting lineup bunts one and swings at three. Out on the pitching mound, catcher-coach Elrod Hendricks hides his stringy body behind an L-shaped protective screen and flips meatballs over the heart of the plate. Most of the hitters gossip around the batting cage as they await their nexts. A few play imaginary base hits. The hitters smile impatiently, flex their bats, and jump in and out of the cage. Hendricks grumbles whenever a batter takes a pitch.

Ken Singleton is the Orioles' cleanup man. At a solid 6′4″ and 210 pounds, he towers Jabbar-like over his teammates. Singleton's handsome face is glazed with a patina of sweat under the glowering July sun. Batting left-handed, Singleton squares and punches a chalk-hugging bunt along the third base line. Then he wraps three straight line drives around the right-field foul pole. Singleton bounces out of the cage and then paces in a slow, thoughtful circle.

"I played hoops in my freshman year at Hofstra University,"

says Singleton, "and there's no doubt that basketball is much more spontaneous than baseball. Baseball keeps on gathering and exploding. Basketball flows. I also think that baseball is more of an individualistic sport than a true team sport. . . . First one guy pitches; then one guy hits; then a fielder does his thing. It's easy to concentrate in baseball because the game is played in little rhythmic spurts. Most of the teamwork in baseball involves only two or three guys at a time, and almost all of it happens on defense. A double play. Or a pick-off at second. There's a lot of defensive teamwork after a base hit with a runner in scoring position. The throw comes in from the outfield, and there's a relay lined up, a cutoff man, guys moving to cover bases, and guys backing up a possible overthrow. But on offense you're up there all by yourself. That's why it's such a drag to be a designated hitter and never play the field."

Singleton pops back into the cage. Before he makes his obligatory bunt, he retrieves a dozen loose baseballs and flips them back to Hendricks. Hendricks holds one in his right hand, two in his glove, and he tosses the rest into a dusty leather ball bag lying at the back of the mound. The Yankees' pitcher is scheduled to be Jim Beattie, a right-handed sinkerballer, so Hendricks grunts and throws a low strike. Singleton uncoils his right hip and opens his body just before the bat slashes across the plate and lines the ball off the top half of the pitching screen. Hendricks doesn't blink. But his next offering is high and tight, and Singleton fouls the ball against the roof of the cage. On his final swing, Singleton snaps out a line drive to left.

"I guess there is a little bit of teamwork on offense." says Singleton. "You can lay down a sacrifice bunt to move a baserunner along. But only when you get the right sign from the coach. . . . Say there's a runner on second and none out, and you hit an easy grounder to the right side that moves the man to third. . . . Well, I guess that's a legitimate sacrifice because you do it on your own and you also get charged with a time at bat. There's only a limited amount of teamwork in baseball, but basketball is the ultimate team game."

While the Oriole hitters hone their offense, Yankee coach Gene Michael perches on the top step of the home team dugout and looks for clues. Michael is 6'2" and a narrow 185 pounds. His sideburns are graying, his face is lean and ascetic, and he denies any knowledge of Basketball Jones. For eight years Michael was a smooth-fielding shortstop and a banjo hitter for the Pittsburgh Pirates, Los Angeles Dodgers, and New York Yankees.

"I played both basketball and baseball back at Kent State," says Michael, "and I was always better in basketball. I was a jump shooter, and I liked to play defense. Then, when I graduated in 1959, the Detroit Pistons offered me a two-year no-cut contract at fifteen thousand a year. At the same time, I was also offered a modest bonus to sign with the Pirates. I was suddenly at a crossroads. . . . I knew that basketball players were closer off the court, and for some reason they always seemed more mature than baseball players. But basketball is grueling, and the physical demands are greater. Baseball players play on a soft turf, so they get fewer injuries and they last longer. Baseball teams also stay in town for three or four days and the traveling is much easier, too. . . . So I signed with the Pirates. Then I spent eight seasons in the minor leagues. In the 'Sally' League, the International League, with Savannah, Grand Forks. I wasn't brought up to the Pirates until 1966, and I immediately found to my regret that I couldn't hit major-league pitching. . . . Now don't get me wrong. . . . I love what I'm doing, and baseball has been very good to me. But looking back, I'd have to say that I made a big mistake."

The Yankees take over the field, and the Orioles slowly swarm to the dugout. Hendricks drops the widemouthed ball bag on the dugout steps and rushes into the clubhouse to take a shower before the game starts. Singleton carefully places his bat in the rack; then he instinctively bends to pick up a loose baseball. Singleton clutches the ball. He drops his glove and springs into a familiar crouch. Singleton pumps a head fake;

then he turns and jump shoots the baseball at the ball bag. "Swish!" he insists, but the ball falls a foot short.

If baseball exhibits too much one-on-one play to be a full-fledged team sport, then the eleven-man full-court mayhem of football certainly qualifies. But like baseball, football is sequential and the spirit of athletic communion flows sporadically. The average NFL contest contains more than 2 hours of measuring, shuttling, huddling, and selling, and only 16.2 minutes of actual ball game. Football teams are also split into defensive and offensive factions which are naturally antagonistic. There are also a variety of kicking units, receiving units, and suicide squads. Football is played by specialists, and some ballplayers never get to touch the ball.

A soccer game generates intense teamwork for 90 minutes and a hockey game for 60. Hockey and soccer both are exquisite team games—hockey players wear red suspenders, and both games work the old "give-and-go." But defense dominates hockey and soccer, and neither sport can approach the equilibrium of basketball.

At latest count, there are 650 ballplayers in major-league baseball, 1,204 players in the NFL, 324 in the NHL, and 242 in the NBA. The eleven-man NBA roster has become the most exclusive in professional sports, and many of today's marginal basketball players would have been All-Stars twenty-five years ago. Unfortunately the superfluity of talent in the NBA has caused most ball clubs to overlook the importance of a well-balanced roster.

From 1976 to 1978 the Philadelphia 76ers were an ill-matched collection of superstars. Starting in the backcourt were Doug Collins at 6'6" and 180 pounds and Henry Bibby at 6'1" and 185 pounds. Collins was a shooting guard who loved to run. But he was too thin to play one-on-one too often, so Collins moved well without the ball and took most of his shots coming off weak-side picks. Despite his lack of bulk, Collins played stubborn defense, but his offense starved whenever his teammates failed to feed him the ball at precisely the right moments. . . . Henry Bibby used to be a shooting guard for UCLA, the Knicks, and the Jazz. His game featured speed and zone-busting 30-foot jumpers; both New York and New Orleans used him as a "sixth man" coming off the bench. At New Orleans, Bibby's career was apparently eclipsed by Pete Maravich. So in 1976, when Philadelphia was looking for warm bodies to flesh out its training camp roster, it bought Bibby for a nominal price. Bibby tried to salvage his career by becoming a ball-handling guard. His conversion was awkward and incomplete, but his sheer willingness to give up the ball made him a starter on a roster overburdened with gunners. . . . Julius Erving started at one forward, operating as a runner, scorer, and penetrator and reinventing the game every time he touched the ball. But alas for his defense. . . . Opposite Erving was George McGinnis, a colossal power forward whose passion was running, dribbling, and forcing shots. . . . Caldwell Jones was the center, a 7'0" defensive dervish whose potent offense was neglected. . . . Everybody on the team loved to run, and Jones was the only starter incapable of triggering a fast break. Whenever the 76ers' running game was clamped, they ostensibly set picks for Collins, sent McGinnis into the pivot, or isolated Erving.

The 76ers usually begin a ball game with a wild shot and an impatient defense. The players clearly mistrust each other, yet they manage to establish a breakneck tempo, and they thunder into an early lead. . . . Steve Mix often replaces George McGinnis late in the first quarter. Mix is a brawling, sweet-shooting, 6'7", 225-pound power forward who delights in playing with his back to the basket. . . . A few minutes later Darryl Dawkins is waved in for Caldwell Jones. Dawkins plays with offensive flair and defensive naïveté and the center's game is turned inside out. . . . Finally, Lloyd Free is buzzed in for Bibby. Free's blitheful, free-lancing is the *causa causans,* and the ball club's fragile rhythm coughs and sputters. . . . The starting five is sifted back into the game, and all the players must struggle to readjust.

"Pass the fuckin' ball, will ya!" Collins screams at McGinnis.

The big man glares at Collins. "Hey, man," McGinnis says, "don't embarrass me like that."

The '76–'77 76ers average a margin of 3.2 points at halftime.

Midway through the third quarter, Lloyd Free tosses a showboat pass into the stands, and coach Billy Cunningham jumps to his feet. "World!" yells Cunningham. "Get under control!"

"I am under control," Free mutters, and the next time he passes the bench he asks to be taken out. The ball game continues as Free and Cunningham swap insults.

With twenty seconds left in the third quarter, Dawkins grabs a defensive rebound and hurls a long outlet pass. "Slow it down!" Cunningham shouts. "Shut the hell up!" Dawkins shouts back.

Free's game is increasingly erratic, and he is sent back to the bench as the last quarter begins. Free slumps down beside assistant coach Chuck Daly. "I'm not playing any more to-night," Free announces. "Unless you put me back in right now."

Sometimes the 76ers won—"I didn't play enough," says McGinnis. Sometimes they lost—"I've got nothing to worry about," says Joe Bryant. "I got my double figures tonight." . . . The 76ers played in chills and fevers, and they never won an important ball game.

The '77–'78 Portland Trail Blazers had much less pure talent than the 76ers, but more more balance: Maurice Lucas and Lloyd Neal were a solid brace of offensive-minded power forwards. Corky Calhoun was a seasoned power forward who concentrated on defense. Bobby Gross and Larry Steele were spirited small forwards, with the 6'5" Steele filling in as a spot-shooting, defensive guard. Dave Twardzik and Johnny Davis provided ball handling and interchangeable unselfishness at one guard position. Lionel Hollins was the scoring guard, and T. R. Dunn was a promising rookie defensive guard. Bill Walton was the only indispensable player, a cosmic defensive center and an elegant passer. Tom Owens was a capable backup center who specialized in passing and playing without the ball.

The role distribution was so ideal that practically any combination of players could produce an obstinate defense and an offense that hummed like a gyroscope. Before Walton fractured a bone in his foot, the '77–'78 Blazers flowed to 50 wins in 60 ball games.

An inkling of Basketball Jones can turn a private half hour of shooting practice into a deep meditation. A full visitation from Basketball Jones reveals the joyful drama of life inside a child's game. Like any other revelation, it appears to different people in different measures:

BOB MCADOO: "The flow of a game means a fast pace when everybody is running. It's the kind of game I like best."

LONNIE SHELTON: "To be in the flow means to completely coordinate your game with your teammates. It means to concentrate, to see everything and to recognize situations as fast as they develop."

DICK MCGUIRE: "There are periods when a team plays well and periods when they play poorly. Peaks and valleys. That's all. 'The flow' is just an expression that sports writers use."

JIM MCMILLIAN: "Being alert to the flow of a basketball

game is a very subtle accomplishment. For players with great natural ability like Bob McAdoo and Julius Erving, the whole concept of the flow has no real meaning. They're so good they can tune in almost any time. But for me, the flow means good timing and execution on both ends of the court. Most of all, it means total unity."

JIM CLEAMONS: "The flow comes from discipline and self-knowledge. It comes from faith in yourself and faith in the team concept. It only happens when you let it happen, not when you try and make it happen. You can always accomplish more when you lose yourself in the flow of a ball game then you can when you think about what you're doing. Playing in the flow is a very spiritual experience."

He who lives by the jump shot dies. But a true vision of Basketball Jones releases the selfless energy that sustains the game, sustains life, and brings them both to victory.